What people are say

The 7 Levels of Wisdom

In her latest book, *The 7 Levels of Wisdom*, author Mónica Esgueva lucidly presents the case for the evolution of consciousness. She offers helpful and practical advice on dealing with our personality disorders in order to open into Pure Consciousness, which transcends our normal dualistic mind. Despite the sad legacy of our past history, this book remains confident that an upward shift in global consciousness is imminent. It is certainly needed!

Jetsunma Tenzin Palmo, Western yogini, teacher of Tibetan Buddhism, and founder of the Dongyu Gatsal Ling Nunnery

A complex and deeply researched examination of how to better understand ourselves and the world around us. *The 7 Levels of Wisdom* is a must-read for all willing to discover our true purpose in life. This book is magnificent.

Paul Zaentz, producer of the film *The English Patient*

In her engaging and well-researched new book, Mónica Esgueva aims to take readers through the gates of wisdom and enable them to find greater fulfillment and peacefulness in their daily lives.

Richard Zimler, bestselling author of *The Last Kabbalist of Lisbon*

Here's to a timeless masterpiece that ushers the reader into an inside-out journey of the depths, breadths, and lengths of not just theoretical knowledge but wisdom in its practicality. Indeed, in a world full of many internal struggles, chaos, and diverse exposure to negativities, Monica has just launched a reset designed to build a new generation of purpose-driven minds ready for tangible positive impact and real-time change. **Eden Benibo**, editor-in-chief of *Hello ICON* magazine

A book like this is so needed in the Western world. A bridge needs to be built, and Mónica Esgueva is the one doing it. **Mynak Tulku Rinpoche**, a spiritual Buddhist leader in Bhutan, ex-director of the National Museum and National Library

The 7 Levels of Wisdom

A Path to Fulfillment

Previous Books

Mindfulness. 2016. Six editions. ISBN-13: 978-8408158554
Cuando sea feliz. 2011. ISBN-13: 979-8525087699
10 claves para alcanzar tus sueños. 2016. ISBN-13: 978-9802716852
El infinito empieza aquí. 2018. ISBN: 840902828X
Los 3 pilares de la felicidad. 2013. ISBN-13: 978-8497546423
Donde pueda rozar tu corazón. 2012. ISBN-13: 978-8492545742
Mensajes para el alma. 2015. ISBN-13: 978-8408125211
Huellas. 2022. ASIN: B09M97DPYP
(All in Spanish)

The 7 Levels of Wisdom

A Path to Fulfillment

Mónica Esgueva

MANTRA
BOOKS

Winchester, UK
Washington, USA

JOHN HUNT PUBLISHING

First published by Mantra Books, 2024
Mantra Books is an imprint of John Hunt Publishing Ltd., No. 3 East Street, Alresford
Hampshire SO24 9EE, UK
office@jhpbooks.com
www.johnhuntpublishing.com
www.mantra-books.net

For distributor details and how to order please visit the 'Ordering' section on our website.

Text copyright: Mónica Esgueva 2023

ISBN: 978 1 80341 470 6
978 1 80341 471 3 (ebook)
Library of Congress Control Number: 2022922705

A CIP catalogue record for this book is available from the British Library.

Design: Lapiz Digital Services

UK: Printed and bound by CPI Group (UK) Ltd, Croydon, CR0 4YY
Printed in North America by CPI GPS partners

We operate a distinctive and ethical publishing philosophy in all areas of our business, from our global network of authors to production and worldwide distribution.

Contents

This book is dedicated to Carlo, the love of my lives.

Acknowledgments

Writing this book was harder than I thought it would be and more rewarding than I could have ever imagined. It all began in the Gobi Desert while I was traveling in Mongolia. The insight came very clearly, and the book had to be written in English to make it as widely available as possible. It has been a long and winding road. The experience has been both internally challenging and fulfilling. Without the guidance, inspiration, and unconditional support from my spiritual Masters and Guides, this book would not exist. They are the foundation of carrying out my mission in this world.

I am eternally grateful to my beloved husband for his unwavering belief in me. His presence in my life is a continuous source of delight, and his patience with me is genuinely admirable. He has an exceptional mind, an unbelievably kind heart, and a remarkable vision. My life has been much better since he arrived.

None of this would have been possible without my parents. I was blessed with amazing parents who stood by me during every struggle and success. They taught me to be fearless and encouraged me to be my own person. I will never be able to thank them enough for everything they have generously done for me.

To all the remarkable spiritual individuals who incarnated on Earth and disinterestedly dedicated their lives to teaching the path of enlightenment and had to suffer rejection, persecution, and ostracism. Their imprints will always be with us. Without their example and wisdom, I would not have been able to learn, integrate, and share what matters the most: developing yourself to reunite with the universal Consciousness. I am forever indebted to them.

Introduction

Consciousness is growing, and the quests of the spirit and heart are expanding. Despite the aggressiveness of the old and outworn consciousness, a new comprehension is setting its path. All the dams can only temporarily hold back this current, and it will be all the more powerful when it breaks through.

Helena Roerich

Although every living thing is somehow aware, only humans are conscious and able to remember, reflect, and self-evolve. We have the potential to become highly developed. However, the reality on our planet is that in one's life, only a few lessons are usually learned. Wisdom is achieved through struggle and sacrifice, and few are willing to give up familiar views and beliefs. Change is therefore met with resistance.

Many people still rely on aggression, jealousy, and violence to compensate for their sense of injustice, lack, and powerlessness because they are on the low end of the evolutionary scale of the development of consciousness. Unfortunately, this is encouraged by the entertainment industry, which often seems to suggest that violence, corruption, and hate are acceptable means to get what you want. Society institutionalizes low emotions that end up ingrained in the unconscious of so many people, becoming an easy target of media, movies, and the internet. Historically, because of this low level of humanity and often unwise leadership, revolutions have meant an uprising of healthy cells for the defense of the whole organism.

Nevertheless, we have free choice, which implies a substantial potential for various experiences and interpretations of what comes to us. As the psychiatrist Viktor Frankl affirmed:

"Everything can be taken from a man but one thing: the last of the human freedoms—to choose one's attitude in any given set of circumstances, to choose one's own way." That freedom is the force that makes us grow internally.

Humans have the luxury of free will, and we can decide our destiny thanks to that. Unfortunately, we seem to be zealously piling up heaps of debris and waste, which will engulf us—literally and metaphorically—if the regeneration of our values does not take place in time.

Every conscious being is in the process of developing and understanding itself all the time. Our growth can occur gradually or suddenly since it is not limited by restraints but by tendencies. Countless options are available for individuals at any time, although they are rarely selected. People tend to take the path of least resistance, supported and appreciated by their environment. Therefore, our range of choices is usually restricted by our perspective of what is possible and what is advisable.

Nowadays, we have access to outstanding amounts of information thanks to the advanced state of technology that was unimaginable only a few decades ago. Nevertheless, information becomes knowledge once we reflect on it, compare it to our experiences and values, and understand it as part of a larger whole. Knowledge only becomes wisdom once we integrate it as part of inner guidance and act coherently with it. Acquiring more knowledge is relatively easy at this point in history. Wisdom is a different matter altogether. True wisdom in a person is recognized by their behavior and presence, without the need to speak much. All the knowledge in the world does not make anyone wise. It can help us become clever, erudite, astute, articulate, fascinating, and so on. And possibly deluded and proud of our expertise, but it does not bring us wisdom automatically. Not until you assimilate that knowledge in such a fashion that you live it. It is not about preaching or showing off what you know, because expertise that does not change our behavior is useless.

An attitude of willingness and earnestness to keep growing and maturing is crucial in assisting an upward movement in consciousness. The motives for change for most people arise when they are seriously challenged through a crisis like an illness, an accident, a divorce, a personal loss, or an essential professional setback. Few people actively choose to keep growing out of an inner drive.

It is also true that nothing grows as slowly as consciousness. It is not enough to explain a new concept or cognitive level; it must be repeated constantly until it is fully integrated into the brain, thanks to brain plasticity. Moreover, only genuine development that is organic and versatile can assure actual development. Nothing can be forced; no step can be taken for granted. The whole process needs to be walked and worked through progressively.

We react to events in a fashion predicated by the level we perceive them from. That is, external circumstances may define conditions, but they do not determine the consciousness level of the person's response. Of course, how we react depends on the world we respond to. But who we become (as well as what goes through our filters of perception) creates the world we believe we are in. For instance, if you believe the world is hostile, you will see life as an endless battle and other people as competitors and enemies; therefore, your behavior will be a continuous confrontation and struggle to defend yourself from possible attacks. Conversely, suppose you believe the world is kind. In that case, you will focus on beauty and kindness and allow yourself to live more peacefully and constructively, creating more positive emotions within yourself and a more positive environment around you.

Our mind engages in denial to protect itself and defend being right no matter what. This provokes resistance to change and prevents our consciousness from advancing much in a lifetime. Only by relinquishing the illusion that we already know everything and by remaining humble can we achieve significant leaps in our level of consciousness. It is easier when we contemplate life as a school. Thus, whatever arises and happens to us is a valuable opportunity to develop. Incredible and painful experiences are not viewed as dramas but as lessons and stepping stones on our path.

As such, mindfulness and meditation help us observe our mind, its tricks and defenses, its biases, its expectations, its desires, its wounds, its judgments, its criticism, its attachments, and so forth. Thus, we no longer function as automatons. A mind that is watched becomes humbler and begins to give up its claims of omniscience. It gives us a chance to increase our level of consciousness by leaving room for an increase in awareness and choice.

As we realize that we are not our minds, thoughts, emotions, past experiences, beliefs, or even dreams, we free ourselves from their grip and domination. We begin to understand that we are not our bodies, possessions, relationships, personality, opinions, or even our history.

Despite its extraordinary importance, one's developmental level is rarely considered in descriptions of human interaction, nor are values, morality, politics, psychology, or behavioral studies. We tend to think that we develop while we are at school. But once that stage is over, adults keep at the same level they reached when they graduated. Most people think there are just three types of humans: children, adolescents, and adults. It is believed that adulthood is simply a stage of life in which we become better at what we do, acquire more skills, and accumulate more knowledge. But in this book, we are talking about making a gradual transformation if we choose to.

Furthermore, this transformation means transitioning to higher stages of development, possessing the traits associated with wisdom and social maturity, becoming increasingly aware of the interconnection of all beings, and becoming more compassionate. So far, we have yet to use a framework for adult development to help us understand where we are and where we want to be. Knowing the different stages can give us a better understanding of ourselves and the people around us. And recognizing that most of us feel a discrepancy between what we value and who we believe we are, and how we actually feel and behave.

Unfortunately, most people are unaware that their developmental perspective influences people's experiences. We do not realize that how we think, how we relate to others, and what motivates us very much depends on our level of development. Expecting a person from one perspective to see the world from another is useless. It is a waste of time to reason another person out of their level of development because they cannot view the world out of their place.

Each perspective has its type of thinking, a way of figuring out what is right or wrong, a way of relating to spiritual matters, a form of understanding yourself, a way of thinking about what is essential and what to believe, a way of dealing with challenges, trials, and pain, and a way of creating particular ways of living life. By exploring this landscape, we can better understand why people have certain behaviors and improve our communication. This also allows us to understand ourselves better and recognize that our perspective is just one of many. We can have a truth, but it is just partial.

Some philosophical and spiritual traditions believe that specific steps are necessary to increase our awareness and develop our level of development. They all include eliminating the identification of self as finite and separated and embracing compassion as our most profound nature, pervading all drives and activity. Being enlightened, and having reached unity with all that there is, is indeed the final goal of our journey, even if it seems like a far-fetched goal in our modern society, which is focused on power, fame, lust, and money.

The power structures are carefully in place to oppress and tyrannize humanity, so we do not have any inclination to listen to the inner voice that leads us out of the Matrix. Nothing new. From the beginning of civilization, society has been erected to the advantage of "the Powers that be." All spheres serve the power Elite, including religion, law, and the arts. What is new is that we have never had an artificially manufactured culture so pervasive and fake. If you do not participate in the twisted game, you will indeed be an outcast with few opportunities to connect with society.

As insidious propaganda has infected all fields to control our minds, mainstream culture is a giant psychological operating machine geared toward keeping people asleep and compliant. The true, the beautiful, and the honorable have lost all value. Now all that matters is what sells, what gets followers, and what increases your popularity and your bank account. It is of no importance if that is shocking, hurtful, negative, or false.

It is difficult to swim in this sea of artifice and mind control. To see through the social engineering and control mechanisms takes a great sense of sovereignty. To go against the powerful currents that drag everybody around takes much courage. To remain authentic to your soul's mission is a titanic task. Committing to shining the Light in such a dark world is something that only heroes do. Use your talents to serve the Light, regardless of the key that will open the pass to higher realms and the new earth.

We are indeed submerged in a Matrix of control. Only that which goes along with the approved beliefs and behavior is allowed. Those considered too independent or subversive are deemed dangerous and labeled as persona non grata. Those who had an advanced level of consciousness and wanted to teach others to liberate themselves from the tethers of oppression were always ostracized or persecuted. Freedom and sovereignty threaten the status quo, and rampant corruption impacts all areas.

The hierarchical system needs to be protected at all costs, so thoughts and behaviors can continue to be imposed, whether directly or subtly. All trends are carefully designed to tell people what to wear, what to do, and how to think. Movies, TV series, YouTube channels, and social media are filtered, so only propaganda and mind-control features make the cut and can expand. Only low-vibrational, harmful, or damaging content can reach significant numbers.

The susceptible population believes that they are free. The reality is that they are paid enslaved people, unable to question anything given to them by authorities or bought-out individuals. They are being primed for a timeline where they become living robots in a metaverse they have willingly consented to.

Nobody is immune to this virus. When the survival impulse, the obsession with fame or wealth, takes over, the individual is prone to take the path of least resistance. That usually means serving the interests of the Powers, even if that entails selling your soul.

We must be aware of how we are prisoners of this perverse game played behind the scenes. We must wake up from our slumber and question what is presented as reality. The time for the graduation of humanity has come, but you will only be ready if you are mature enough to see through the lies of the only approved narrative. People have to grow up and stop believing that the Powers that be do care for their welfare. Only children believe in Santa Claus. Although we are raised to obey authorities and think that experts are always right, we must be sovereign individuals to move to the next stage of human evolution. Being a puppet of mainstream propaganda keeps you in a conventional, given way of thinking. People are kept hopelessly enslaved by giving them the illusion that they are free. Even in liberal Western democracies, being free is utterly delusional. As long as you cannot think for yourself and are influenced by the pressures of society, you will be another obedient soldier of the Matrix.

Sovereignty with an increased level of consciousness is the only solution to the current chaos and degradation. If we want to survive as a species and thrive as human beings, we must take charge of our own life. Without an urgent modification of our perspective, interests, values, and ways of life, we are heading toward a dead end on this planet. In short, the current system based on indoctrination and financial slavery is moving human society closer to collapse.

There is no place left to hide in the world. Therefore, the essential oneness of everything and the interconnectivity of it all is not just a spiritual teaching but an obvious truth for all to see.

The current planetary situation is very different from the last century's. When World War II took place, there was a localized tumor that we had to extirpate, and it was done that way. Our current circumstances are more similar to cancer that has spread throughout the body and requires unique healing methods. There is rampant corruption in all spheres of life. Public life—from politicians to pharmaceutical companies to celebrities—is based on deceit. People are so out of touch with their inner guidance that they accept mainstream news and threats as real gospel. Simple goals are endlessly sublimated by social media. Relentless stress is compensated for with ubiquitous distractions. Obsession with productivity is sold as the meaning of life. Functional pain that warns us of our incoherence is numbed with many addictions. There is such a cacophony of aggressive inputs surrounding us that the only escape is running faster toward destruction.

We have arrived at a time when a new evolutionary leap in consciousness and culture is required. The global challenges we face require a higher level of consciousness to realize that what unites us is much greater than what divides us. In the current situation, the human race urgently needs more individuals to develop wisdom for the benefit of all. No isolated approach will get us far. Only a Unitive view that recognizes that everything is interdependent will help us take a positive step forward. A Unitive view will help us realize that we belong to a unity of biological kinship and that we also belong to one single system of evolution.

We know now that more of what we already have will not change how we feel or fill the vacuum within our souls. Advanced technology in the hands of an egotistical Elite will end up in a new world order where a mighty handful of individuals will play god with the sleeping masses.

Focusing on endless increases in profits without considering the welfare of all beings on Earth will leave millions starving while very few become useless billionaires. Fixation with short-term financial gains and maximization of return is seriously degrading the future of the next generations. We have participated in an erosive global economy where 62 individuals have as much wealth as half the world's population. As we face an abyss, we have reached a time in our history when a drastic turn is imperative. We have to choose. The time of the separation of the wheat from the chaff has come. Each person must decide where he or she wants to be: living in an organic timeline with brotherhood and compassion as the norm, or being willing to be dragged into a transhumanist timeline where the only freedom allowed would be scoring points in the metaverse. Those who rely on their own free will and are aligned with the love and service vibration will live in the former. Those who act as sheep are wholly programmed to follow the orders of their evil shepherd.

Unless we understand the urgency of our situation and take responsibility for ourselves and future generations, this will have a bleak way out. This turn has nothing to do with having a different party in government, changing our institutions, or stopping planned pandemics. The change must come from an increased consciousness on the level of individuals and must be bottom-up for it to transform our world. Nobody is going to save us from our predicaments. Although help is always readily available in a conscious and loving universe, it is up to each person to choose the pace of their evolution. As we will see in this book, the only way forward and upward is through wisdom and compassion. We develop by redirecting our life purpose to helping others and contributing to a better world. We truly progress when we can adopt the role of the witness who sees with clarity and without emotional reaction.

Real wisdom is the application of knowledge, intelligence, experience, and creativity aligned with values toward achieving a common good. True wisdom is not about maximizing one's own or others' self-interests but about balancing those interests within oneself to prioritize the larger aim of contributing to the welfare and wellbeing of others.

Over the past 25 years, I have observed that the Eastern way is not typically resonant with Westerners, mainly because there is a clash between the Western mindset and the current environment of modern society. We must acknowledge that those Eastern philosophies and religions were designed for the Eastern mind and culture. As psychiatrist Carl Jung said: "Westerners cannot slap Eastern spirituality on top of a Western ego and expect enlightenment." Only a small number of people are willing to do thousands of prostrations and chant mantras they do not understand, visualize foreign deities in their meditation, learn traditional scriptures by heart, or withdraw from the mundane world to join an ashram, or seek a guru and follow his instructions to the letter. However, more and more people in the West have questions that cannot be answered by materialism or science. Money, possessions, and relationships are not the solutions people used to think they were—they are not enough to fill the vacuums. More people are looking for a more profound and expansive lifestyle. More people are unhappily witnessing the lack of justice around them and are opening their hearts and minds to a more compassionate way of living. More and more people are becoming interested in inner transformation. Those people are the ones getting ready for the new earth.

Eastern traditions have much to teach us, especially considering the amount of time, energy, and effort they have dedicated to spiritual realization over hundreds of years. It might be worthwhile to adjust the Eastern way to appeal to the Western intellect and current circumstances since people may be more inclined to consider reaching the highest levels of human consciousness as the most crucial objective. Regardless of their responsibilities and life conditions, they must see it as feasible. The new stage of evolution is ready for the part of humanity who wish to take this unique opportunity and take a leap. This book is written for those individuals.

Part I

Why wisdom?

An aimless life is always a miserable life.

Every one of you should have an aim. But do not forget that the quality of your life will depend on the quality of your aim.

Your aim should be high and wide, generous and disinterested; this will make your life precious to yourself and others.

But whatever your ideal, it cannot be perfectly realized unless you have realized perfection in yourself.

Sri Aurobindo

Chapter 1

The crucial importance of wisdom

Just as treasures are uncovered from the earth, so virtue appears from good deeds, and wisdom appears from a pure and peaceful mind. To walk safely through the maze of human life, one needs the light of wisdom and the guidance of virtue.

Buddha

Throughout the ages, wisdom has been considered the pinnacle of insight into human development and the means and ends of a good life. The West's most comprehensive view of wisdom comes mainly from philosophy. To have a clearer idea, let's see what it represents:

1. A truly superior level of knowledge, judgment, and advice.
2. It addresses fundamental and complex questions and strategies about the conduct and meaning of life.
3. It includes awareness about the limits of knowledge and the world's uncertainties.
4. It entails understanding with extraordinary scope, depth, measure, and balance.
5. It involves a perfect synergy of mind and character, considering all virtues.
6. It represents knowledge used for the good or wellbeing of oneself and others.

According to the first philosophers, wisdom meant knowledge about the world as a whole and of the truth and the Divine. Back then, striving to attain wisdom was the purpose of human ambition. And it was made explicit that the goal was orchestrating mind and virtue together toward human excellence and the common good.

In psychology, Jung and Erikson defined wisdom as the final stage of personality development, achieved only by some people in late adulthood. For them, wisdom is attained due to a long-term personality development process in the third part of life. It is related to a detached concern with life in the face of death. It is also connected with the acceptance of our existence, which is a consequence of a positive balance and finding a purpose in life.

Generally, Western theories tend to focus more on knowledge and analytic ability. However, wisdom only appears when understanding is realized through reflection on personal experiences when it transforms the person and contributes to a positive change in the world. Intellectual and theoretical knowledge that does not benefit society has nothing to do with wisdom. It necessarily implies a development of the cosmic outlook, which encompasses the whole of reality.

Wise people can balance personal and interpersonal interests, short- and long-term, intellectual and intuitive knowledge, personal experience, and a strong base of values to guide their actions for the common good.

Recent studies have shown that countless people in our society think that wisdom is equivalent to intelligence and logic, and most people do not even consider that the meaning of life is an essential part of it. Conditioned by our materialistic culture, we tend to believe that achieving our objectives is crucial for wisdom. Regardless of the common good as an essential aim.

Therefore, there is much confusion between knowledge and wisdom, thinking that the former can be a substitute for the latter. We lack the awareness that learning is associated with: acting for global welfare, deep and conscious reflection of value systems and how to materialize them with coherent actions, and appreciation of the limits of logical and analytical knowledge to grow as individuals and create a better world. That is why we (urgently) need to make society aware of the importance of wisdom as well as the methods of its development. Given the current state of affairs on our planet, we have to act differently before the same egocentric, egotistic, hedonistic, and superficial way of living destroys the earth and our humanity with it.

To make it more understandable, we can distinguish three basic dimensions of wisdom.

The first is cognitive, and it entails being able to thoroughly understand situations, as well as the positive and negative aspects of human nature, being aware of life's inherent uncertainty and the ability to make the most beneficial decision, having rich knowledge of life, tolerance of ambivalence, recognizing one's limits, and seeing reality beyond one's projections. Being intelligent is therefore necessary, but not sufficient.

The second has to do with taking the time to reflect with serenity, being able to handle multiple perspectives, learning from past experiences, having a sound judgment about complex issues, respect for differences among others, having a sense of justice, self-insight, taking responsibility for your own life and feelings, empathy, openness to new experiences, a sense of humor, resilience and social cooperation.

The third has to do with what we could call spirituality: altruism, other-centeredness, willingness to forgive, kindness, and compassion for other beings... As well as possessing mature and self-transcendent characteristics such as integrity, inner peace, humility, gratitude, self-compassion, mindfulness, respect for nature, nonviolence, ethical conduct, deep acceptance of death... And last but not least, a general sense of psychological wellbeing (without lingering wounds), life satisfaction, and having a purpose in life.

It seems that the process of aging itself provides many of the conditions in which wisdom can conceivably flourish: a good number of experiences to reflect on, a tendency to seek meaning within instead of outside, a greater openness to paradox and contradiction, and a general physical slowdown that makes the person more aware of his or her limits and the reality of mortality, as well as more time to be more philosophical. However, do we have to wait until we retire to get to this point? Shouldn't we start this task exactly where we are? By doing so, wouldn't we enhance the quality of our lives and choices, as well as our inner depth and serenity? Wouldn't we start changing the world if each of us were to take responsibility for it right now and start modifying the egocentric and survival perspective to include others and the way we are all interrelated?

Chapter 2

Stages of development

Nobody can act beyond their level of consciousness.

Eckhart Tolle

Adult human development has been researched for over 50 years. It is now an accepted fact that most capacities of human beings grow through several distinct stages of psychological maturity. In each stage, a different way of looking at the world occurs. Yet, despite this enormous body of evidence, our culture seems to know almost nothing about human development, at least as it pertains to adults. We have yet to fully integrate the notion that adulthood is a development period. It is not just for kids and unstable teenagers; we are talking about a lifelong journey. In social and psychological studies, some scholars have designed human development models to help understand those stages individuals go through, representing a fundamental shift in their worldview, their way of making sense, self-perspective, and moral reasoning.

How we see ourselves and how we understand our life is about shifts as we move through developmental stages. Our relationships, values, existence, and sense of self adjust and change as we grow. Development and growth proceed in a sequence of continuums, chronologically ordered phases that cannot be rearranged. Although not all individuals go through the steps at the same rate, nobody can skip or leap from one stage to the next. All people have to go through the same stages in the same order; it is impossible to enter a later phase without going through an earlier one. Each senior dimension transcends but includes its junior. There is a hierarchy of evolution, as we cannot have wholeness without it. Each level represents an increase in complexity, perfection, and integrative capacity over its predecessors. Higher development always means the possibility of higher or more universal integration. This framework reflects the nature of reality as it is, where we can recognize diverse levels of existence. As thought leader Ken Wilber expresses it, "They range from matter to body to mind to soul to spirit."

Behaviors at one stage are perceived to be qualitatively different, not just more of the same. The changes are always gradual and, in specific terms, continuous. However, developmental progression involves not only growth but usually complete disorientation to make way for a different and renovated orientation. We can clearly understand it by reflecting on how we perceived ourselves and our world differently at 30 versus 15 years old. Our worldview develops over time to become more inclusive and expansive. The meaning we attribute to life is determined by the lens through which we perceive the world and ourselves. The thicker the lens, the less capacity we have to hold ourselves apart from the object of our perceptions (including thoughts and emotions).

Stages or periods can be split up conceptually in any number of ways. I will present the most relevant for our topic. As we evolve to more mature stages, it marks who we are, what we value, and how we make meaning. Our choices and actions change. They become increasingly sophisticated, subtle, and inclusive.

Piaget was one of the first theorists to propose a detailed stage model. He explored how children and adolescents make sense of their experiences across several domains, covering four universal cognitive stages. Before Piaget's work, the common assumption in psychology was that children were less competent thinkers than adults. Piaget showed that young children think in strikingly different ways compared to adults.

He emphasized the importance of schemas in cognitive development. A schema can be defined as a set of linked mental representations of the world, which we use to understand and respond to situations. The assumption is that we store these mental representations and apply them when interacting with our environment, which influences how we interpret reality.

Development is biologically based, and changes as the child matures. Each child goes through the stages in the same order, and no stage can be missed (although some people may never attain the latter stages). There are individual differences in the rate at which children progress through stages. Piaget did not claim that a particular stage was reached at a certain age, although descriptions of the stages often indicate the age at which the average child would reach it. For him, development was not a gradual accumulation of new knowledge but rather a process of moving through different stages of reasoning in which knowledge is transformed.

Robert Kegan went beyond children and adolescents to study adults, and beyond the study of cognition to include emotions. He also looked at the role of social context and cultural demands. For Kegan, the process of growth involves an evolution of meaning marked by continual shifts from periods of stability to periods of instability, leading to the ongoing reconstruction of the relationship of individuals with their environment. Growth involves movement through progressively more complex ways of knowing, including cognitive, personal, and relationship modifications.

Kegan saw the development process as an effort to resolve the tension between a desire for differentiation and an equally powerful desire to be immersed in one's surroundings. He stated that growth could be painful since it involves changing one's way of functioning in the world.

In his model, two adult developmental stages take us past the stage emerging in adolescence, adopting and internalizing the values of society. The first adult stage emerges in the thirties, and then passes to the last stage, appearing at around 50 years old.

In our modern age, we need to pass the limiting mindset that adopts the values of its society from the inside and is subject to them as unquestioned assumptions. We have to be able to adapt to changing conditions without depending on gaining acceptance by following the rules of our group.

In the twenty-first century, we require more flexibility to step back and see our culture from the outside, allowing each person to evaluate, criticize, and perceive ways to improve the world. Rules and mores of our social group are no longer unquestionable assumptions but can be assessed and modified.

At the last stage of development, as designed by Kegan, people reach a mindset that allows a person to step back from any one culture and see his or her social group as just one possibility among many. To survive the current difficulties, we will need leaders at all levels who work with and around the other mindsets, not just cater to them. We require more people who challenge the myths and assumptions that are laying waste to the world. We need more people who can honestly see that it takes a higher stage of mind to understand that at the root of every social and political problem we face lies the concept that people have difficulties seeing and taking others' perspectives. No one society or economic system has all the answers, and we must stop punishing people who think differently. For the first time in our history, a globalized world confronts us with a task for which only people with self-transforming minds are well-equipped: becoming aware that there are diverse value systems suitable for different occasions and different people, and becoming comfortable with contradictions in those value systems.

Jane Loevinger's fascinating theory of ego development is possibly the most comprehensive in psychology. She also provides a framework for understanding the growth of a person's way of constructing meaning throughout their life. For her, higher stages represent greater ability to deal with complexity and a broader, deeper, and more integrated perspective.

For Loevinger, each stage represents a rearrangement of the self-system toward greater self-awareness and relationship awareness, less defensiveness, more capacity to hold complexity, increased flexibility, more reflective ability, more autonomy, greater tolerance for difference and ambiguity, and more concern for others.

Tiers of human development

Developmental theorists have grouped the different stages into some significant blocks that highlight the most critical shifts in the evolution of human consciousness. These basic tiers are:

1. Pre-conventional. This includes those stages of development that come before a person enters society. It is characterized by unclear boundaries of a separate self and not full use of rational thought processes.
2. Conventional. Here the person is influenced and defined mainly by the constraints of society and identifies with a separate self, using a rational and objective mind all the time.
3. Post-conventional. The person can move outside—as well as questioning—conventional rules. She also identifies with a self more extensive than her own physical body and starts exploring ways beyond the rational mind.

Although there is evidence that consciousness level stabilizes for most individuals by early adulthood, clusters of transformative life experiences and the midlife crisis can lead to self-doubt and personal questioning. A marriage crisis, a career burnout, or a serious disease could be a catalyst for development.

In some cases, certain personality elements may enhance or constrain consciousness development by influencing the degree of exposure to potentially unbalancing life experiences, but this could be adjusted by assimilation or accommodation instead. Attitudes such as openness, self-acceptance, flexibility, tolerance of complexity and ambiguity, empathy, resiliency, a wish to grow, and internal locus of control may amplify the potential for development.

Susanne Cook-Greuter later expanded and revised Loevinger's model, based on the findings of thousands of interviews, presenting fascinating information about how humans grow internally throughout life. Therefore, the stages she describes are not theoretical. Instead, they are derived from actual data from real people, and thus, they come from analysis of that data compiled over many decades. In this book, we will take her model as the main base, as it shows how humans make meaning as we develop, how our sense of identity evolves (considering both the strengths and limits of each stage of development), as well as describing the challenges individuals need to overcome to move to the next stage of development.

How do we then ascend from one stage to the next?

Inner growth proceeds by shedding one worldview about reality and adopting another. Only when the environment fails to meet one's expectations can actual development occur. Thus, previous meanings are stripped away and new approaches to life must be considered. Usually, it takes years of putting experiences into context before a transformation occurs. Typically, when the individual is presented with a life dilemma containing factors that create dissonance and imbalance with his current paradigm, the person cannot integrate those new elements in the same previous fashion. Thus, he is forced to question and release his current views and begins to embrace a higher-level perspective. However, the last two stages (Alchemist and

Unitive) are somewhat different. There, the person becomes the seeker, who desires to perceive beyond his current model of reality. In other words, he grows through a series of incidents or revelations that are frequently self-induced. Often, a spiritually oriented event triggers the final release into the highest level of consciousness.

Chapter 3

Maslow's legacy

Most of the luxuries and many of the so-called comforts of life are not only not indispensable, but positive hindrances to the elevation of mankind.

Henry David Thoreau

Abraham Maslow (1908–70) was one of the most influential psychologists of modern times. He believed that humans had great potential. He thought there was more to humans than rewards, punishments, and subconscious urges. To Maslow, people were full of positive potential. He developed humanistic psychology (together with Carl Rogers), which focuses on people's potential to become all they can be. Other psychologists helped develop different elements, but he is primarily considered the father of the humanist movement in psychology.

Maslow's hierarchy of human needs is one of his most enduring contributions to psychology. In his motivational scheme, as constructed by him, he described how human needs are arranged in a hierarchy. A person must complete one level of the hierarchy to move on to the next, although not all people move through all stages. I have wanted to add a sixth level (not usually included in the standard versions) since it shows a more accurate model, considering his later work and private journal entries. It is depicted as follows:

1. Physiological (survival) needs: seeks to obtain the necessities of life.
2. Safety needs: seeks security through order and law.

3. Belongingness and love need: seeks affiliation with a group.
4. Esteem needs: seeks esteem through recognition or achievement.
5. Self-actualization: seeks fulfillment of personal potential.
6. Self-transcendence: seeks to further a cause beyond the self and to experience a communion beyond the boundaries of the self through peak experiences.

Maslow gave the human need for self-actualization special attention. He selected 48 extraordinary human beings for his study on self-actualization and then described the patterns common to all. He concluded that the highest human values are associated with self-actualization. That is, striving for health, searching for identity and autonomy, and yearning for excellence. It is the need for the development of the essential human nature; a thrust toward a unified personality, toward "spontaneous expressiveness," toward identity and complete individuality, "toward seeing the truth rather than being blind," toward being good rather than evil, and toward creativeness.

For Maslow, spiritual life constitutes the essential trait of humanity. He discovered that two sets of forces pull at the individual. On the one hand, pressures toward health and self-actualization. And on the other, regressive pressure backward in the direction of weaknesses and sickness. When neuroses are related to "spiritual disorders," they bring loss of meaning, anger, and grief over lost love, loss of hope and courage, despair over the future, perceiving that one's life is being wasted, and the impossibility of joy or love. These are failures to measure up to full humanness.

As Maslow characterizes them in his *Journals* (1969), Transcenders go beyond the basic needs and love the ultimate good things, excellence, perfection, and a good job. They identify with the cosmos and feel they belong to it by right (cosmic consciousness). They sacralize life, transcend the ego, and are motivated by more impersonal goals. Furthermore, they have transcendent objectivity and thus observe reality better. They also go beyond deciding and choosing. They are more attuned to letting the universe (from which they no longer feel separated) decide and letting the flow take them. Not only that, but they are no longer preoccupied with their uniqueness and security since they are beyond selfishness and extreme individuality.

At the level of self-actualization, the individual works to actualize his or her potential. Thus, there is a specific self-aggrandizing aspect to this motivational stage, as there is with all the steps below. At the level of self-transcendence, the individual's own needs are secondary, to a great extent, in favor of service to others and some higher force or cause conceived outside the personal self.

The crucial issue is the dominant motivation at work in the person's life. All people experience hunger; however, hunger is the defining experience only for individuals centered on the physiological or survival level of Maslow's hierarchy of needs. So for him, the experience of transcendence is one thing, and having one's motivational life centered on self-transcendence is entirely another.

Maslow claimed that people are oriented toward either growth or safety in their everyday lives. A growth orientation facilitates more effective psychological health and wellbeing. He also elaborated on the desire for self-fulfillment that is the essence of human drives (albeit at the top of the needs) and what ultimately drives a person to become actualized in what they can potentially be. To have a more precise idea of what having self-actualizing experiences entails, here is a summary in his words:

- Experiencing fully, vividly, selflessly, with complete and total absorption

- Making the progression choice in a given moment rather than the regression choice, the growth choice instead of the fear choice
- Letting the self emerge by listening to one's inner voice, instead of our parents' voices or that of the establishment, authority, or tradition
- Being honest rather than not, taking responsibility for one's beliefs and perspectives
- Being courageous, not afraid, daring to be different, unpopular, nonconformist
- Using one's intelligence to go through an arduous and demanding period of preparation to bring to fruition one's possibilities
- Setting up the conditions so that peak experiences are more likely to occur—by getting rid of false notions, for instance
- Identifying one's defenses and finding the courage to give them up.

Maslow eventually began to distinguish between non-transcending self-actualizers (people who are essentially more practical, realistic, mundane, capable, and secular people, doers rather than meditators, practical and pragmatic rather than aesthetic, reality-cognitive rather than emotional and experiencing) and transcending self-actualizing individuals who exhibit a Unitive perception and a fusion of the eternal with the temporal, the sacred with the profane. Maslow thought that self-actualization was not enough for a complete picture of the optimally functioning human being. The humanist psychologist gave examples of the former: Mrs. Eleanor Roosevelt, Harry Truman, and Eisenhower. And of the latter, Aldous Huxley and Einstein.

In fact, during the last three years of his life, Maslow recognized that transpersonal psychology was a separate force from the humanistic approach, as self-transcendence differs from self-actualization. He conceptualized self-transcendence as seeking a benefit beyond the purely personal, looking for communion with the transcendent, perhaps through mystical or transpersonal experiences, identifying with something more significant than the purely individual self, often engaging in service to others. He even modified his motivational model of the hierarchy of needs to include this additional level. While the earlier model positions the highest form of motivational development as individuals with a well-adjusted and fulfilled person, the later model places the highest level as a transpersonal one, where the self and its needs are transcended.

To make it more straightforward, we will present a compiled set of qualities that, in Maslow's opinion, distinguished transcending self-actualizers from non-transcending ones. Here are some of the characteristics of those transcenders:

- Peak experiences become essential things in their lives, the most precious aspects of life.
- They speak naturally and unconsciously the language of poets, mystics, seers, and people who live under the perspective of eternity, the language of parable and paradox.
- They perceive the sacred within the secular, the sacredness in all things, and at the same time, act at the practical and everyday level.
- They are motivated by the values of perfection, truth, beauty, goodness, unity, and transcendence.
- They recognize each other and establish almost instant intimacy and mutual understanding even upon first meeting.
- They are more responsive to beauty; indeed, they tend to see beauty in everything.

- They are more holistic about the world. They see humanity as one, and limiting concepts such as national interest or the family's religion cease to exist for them.
- They transcend the ego and the identity with it more often and more efficiently.
- Not only are such people lovable, but they are also more awe-inspiring, more "unearthly," and more easily admired.
- They are far more apt to be innovators, discoveries of the new, what could be, and what exists in potential.
- They can be more ecstatic yet more prone to cosmic sadness over people's stupidity, cruelty to each other, and blindness.
- They consider the less-developed brother a member of the family who must be loved and cared for regardless of what he does because he is, after all, a family member.
- They find mystery attractive rather than frightening. Instead of pursuing knowledge to reduce anxiety, they take it with a sense of awe, humility, ultimate ignorance, and reverence.
- They have a greater understanding of apparent evil, so it generates greater compassion in them and a less ambivalent and more decisive fight against it.
- They are more apt to regard themselves as instruments of the transpersonal and temporary custodians of greater intelligence. That entails a kind of detachment toward themselves that might sound like arrogance or grandiosity to others.

While self-actualizers have strong identities, they know who they are, where they are going, what they want, and what they are suitable for, and they use themselves well and authentically and according to their true nature. Transcenders are this and more than this because, for them, it is easier to transcend their ego, the self, and the narrow identity.

They are more Taoistic: they see everything as miraculous, perfect, just as it should be. Therefore, it breeds less impulse to push for anything; they do not consider that everything needs to be improved or intruded upon.

Part II

The 7 levels of wisdom

Most human beings today waste some 25 to 30 years of their lives before they break through the actual and conventional lies which surround them.

Isadora Duncan

Humans develop through a series of internal stages that progressively refine our maturity. We all share this odyssey of traveling uphill through all the different stages until we reach unity with all that is. A baby only follows survival impulses, and then, as a toddler, it knows only its ego. The young adult learns to appreciate their narrow social group. And hopefully, at some point, they will be able to transcend this and enlarge their perspective globally, beyond the social group. And in the end, fully integrate the intimate relationship with all sentient beings.

Moving through stages also involves encompassing more consciousness, awareness, and compassion. We could say that what changes through the different stages is the person's operating system—keeping in mind that any progression and evolution needs to include that which went before. That is the only way to transcend a previous stage. None of these stages is better or worse than the others. They are simply rungs of development that all of us have the potential to experience. If anything, we place more value on one another solely because, with each higher level, a person gains a more inclusive perspective and a more beneficial impact on others, especially in the final stages. Evolution is intrinsically purposeful but not linear; it is somewhat complex and involves a lot of back and forth.

Moreover, each stage describes an ideal result, and we rarely fit every aspect of the descriptions. The stages serve more as a road map, designed as a way for us to familiarize ourselves with how we currently experience reality and help us navigate the terrain of being human. They can clarify our current orientation and what awaits us. This can also help us understand and relate to other people with greater empathy and effectiveness and offer an inspiring view of our collective human evolutionary potential.

Our center of gravity and, therefore, the lens of each stage ultimately affects how our view of the world is interpreted, what we can be aware of, how we make decisions, and how we behave. Research shows that the surrounding culture and friends, historical times, societal norms and awards, and our life circumstances greatly influence this. All these can be limiting or growth-stimulating elements that most impact our developmental progression. The framework presented here can offer a chance to understand how people interpret events and how they may respond in certain circumstances. It can benefit those dedicated to lifelong learning, so they can embrace this knowledge to become more self-aware and transform their ability, and that of those around them, to thrive. It can also serve us to pay attention to which stage we are at. We can only deliberately work to change our perspective, thoughts, feelings, and actions. Please remember that our stage of development is mainly a filter; it is not who we are.

For clarity, I want to mention that hardly any people develop to the upper realms of this spectrum. The greatest obstacle for humans on the way to evolution is the solitary struggle we must go through to discover our light and inner peace. Most people take a position and stay there all their life rather than moving on. This happens for a variety of reasons that I will explain later. Like in nature, few seeds sprout, and only a handful can bear fruit.

Why do we have to keep growing to higher ground? And what is the point of all this development if ultimately life is an illusion or *maya*, as Shakespeare pointed out, "All the world is a stage, and all the men and women merely players"? I guess it depends on our tolerance for suffering. If the person can endure a high degree of suffering without flinching, there is no point in wanting to keep evolving. If, on the other hand, the person is fed up with feeling trapped in a wheel of hardships, endless conflicts, non-stop battles, ubiquitous dissatisfaction, and profound inner vacuum... Then he may want to take steps to liberate himself. Fortunately, some paths allow us to free ourselves. It is only when we are tired of being subjugated and tortured that we are willing to take them consciously and climb the ladder.

At these challenging times of widespread anxiety, when so many things seem to be falling apart, fear can tempt us to get stuck in our convictions. During this chaotic transitional period, there is an urgent need to transcend ego-centered views and approach the situation from a broader, healthier perspective. That allows us to appreciate the contributions of all other levels and then move forward with an inclusive dialogue around our challenging modern problems. A non-dogmatic spirituality filled with compassion will be the avenue by which many can progress. The leap required for our new era must come from the heart rather than being merely cognitive. Ultimately, from the evolutionary perspective, the only sustainable solution not to repeat the mistakes humanity has been trapped into is a global shift to a new consciousness.

Chapter 4

Starting to integrate experiences

Contrary to most professional opinion, a gnawing dissatisfaction with life is not a sign of mental illness, nor an indication of poor social adjustment, nor a character disorder...A person who is beginning to sense the suffering of life is beginning to awaken to deeper realities, truer realities.

Ken Wilber

Wisdom cannot be acquired until a certain threshold has been passed, mainly having left behind the more childish stages in which a person is only concerned about his safety and meeting basic needs and moves impulsively toward these ends. In those earlier stages, relationships with others are limited to what they can provide to meet one's needs. The main concern is impulse gratification. The sense of self is more visceral than intellectual, mainly reactive and automatic. The person is interested in power in service of his own self-centered objectives. He sees the world only in terms of his demands and wants, and is ready to control or manipulate others to get what he wants. A person at this stage values uniformity. There is an impulse to resist the will of others, test limits, and assert his control. The world is a hostile and dangerous place. Rules are recognized but only followed for immediate advantage or to avoid punishment. The person does not feel responsible for any failure or trouble he may cause because he does not understand the connection between action and consequences. The individual blames others for his shortcomings as a way to protect himself. It corresponds to the 'pre-conventional' tier, which includes around 10% of the

Western adult population. I will not elaborate much more on this first block as it is not our primary focus of interest.

At the 'conventional' tier (approximately 75% of the population in Western nations), people are concerned with gaining more knowledge about how to work effectively in the world. Progress is defined by discovering more pieces of the puzzle: distinguishing patterns, rules, and laws that govern how things work; learning to predict better, measure, and explain the world; appreciating and considering a more extensive time stretch—in other words, increasing knowledge and taking more ownership of one's life. Social maturity stops here; beyond this tier most adults do not progress.

Now, I will present the seven levels, from the lowest to the most developed.

1. Conformist (approximately 12% of the population in Western nations). Most people have reached this stage by age 12, though some adults remain here. In healthy development, this is the stage of early adolescence, though many people get stuck in this stage throughout life. Their relationship with a group defines their self-identity. This leads to confused boundaries between oneself and the group (whether family, team, or nation). Conformists do not take the initiative but rather seek to listen to and follow the culture—pleasing others, seeking acceptance, and deferring to the group and cultural norms. They accept norms and roles without questioning them. They live based on rules and "shoulds" and identify with those who share their tastes and perspectives. Furthermore, they dislike standing out and tend to give up the responsibility for making choices to leaders within the group. The price for protection is loyalty and obedience.

For them, being friendly, pleasant, and good-looking is fundamental. People are judged by how they look, so they worry about what others think and feel at any moment. They tend to accept norms without question. Their cognitive system is divided into simple categories and types of people based on external distinctions. They give lots of advice, telling others what to do or not to do.

They are identified with and bound to those with the same tastes, beliefs, characteristics, and aims, and they get confused or threatened by differing perspectives, demands, or diversity.

2. Expert (approx. 30% of the population in Western nations). These individuals need to differentiate themselves from the immediate family context and express and uphold their newly discovered independence. They want to see themselves as unique. Unlike Conformists, they do not mind asserting their needs and wants. However, now they would like to be accepted by others because of their difference. They also usually want to be better than others and stand out from the crowd.

Individuals at this stage try to exert control by perfecting their knowledge in their personal and professional lives. They tend to adhere to a particular ideology or theory they defend wholeheartedly. Experts need to have the last word, a competitive one-upmanship. They believe they know all the answers, feel righteous, and often view others as being in the wrong. Others are evaluated according to their capabilities and standards. Severe criticism of how another thinks is a common form of intellectual aggression here. A sense of superiority is not very well hidden. They discredit material that does not fit into their frame by dismissing it or belittling others. They typically have a wicked sense of humor.

They are concerned with fulfilling their responsibilities and duties and frequently have compulsive and perfectionist tendencies. While there is a cognitive capacity to look inside, their defense tends to be ultra-rational. They live in a world where things are sure and clear, and they feel entitled to impose their views on others. Experts run most cultures.

3. Achiever (approximately 30% of the population in Western nations). This is considered the highest adult stage in Western cultures, and society supports, promotes, and rewards its achievements. It is a necessary precondition for democracy since it requires citizens capable of rational deliberation and choice to shelter the whole while allowing the law to reflect changes.

People here strive to reach their goals; they use their own standards and are self-critical. They have principles they believe in. They cultivate relationships and can recognize multiple perspectives and possibilities. They are interested in receiving feedback that will help them improve and achieve their goals, but they tend to reject (or even dislike) feedback that challenges how they operate. Engaged in their projects, they hardly slow down to look at the present moment and reflect upon life more deeply.

They have a great capacity to handle data and make systematic and rational sense of their experience. In Western society, we call it "objectivity." However, just because you can take everything together in a coherent scheme does not make it a truthful reflection of reality. Once you realize this, you can evolve from the self-authoring self to the one who can transform himself. Only when you can embrace contradiction and apparent opposition can you hold multiple systems of thinking. Only then can you understand that the self is not something to identify with and defend at all costs but a fluid perception in constant change.

Achievers can belong to diverse groups simultaneously with different agendas and styles without feeling torn between them or confused regarding competing loyalties. Social contacts have become increasingly varied and rich. Others are appreciated for having additional expertise as long as they do not interfere with their beliefs and values. Their loyalty is given to a chosen belief system rather than the individuals leading them.

They are interested in reasons, causes, goals, effects, and the effective use of time. Achievers may also become interested in the truth about themselves through feedback and introspection. They generally have positive self-regard based on their successes, their ability to master their lives, and their sense of independence. Their self-esteem depends more on achieving their goals and less on external affirmation and approval.

At this stage, there is the belief in the possibility of reaching perfection and the scientific method to discover the truth: how things are and the essence of human nature. They are interested in analyzing and improving their methods of inquiry and measuring. They are committed to achieving results with responsibility and efficiency. There is a need to excel and be better than others. It is important to be admired for their achievements. They often have a desire for recognition. They may have a driven quality to accomplish something in this world or to improve the world versus the need for later stages to develop themselves. They have a sense of responsibility and obligation toward others, even while pursuing their own goals and agendas.

Research has shown that most adults stabilize at the conventional tier. This is well below the maximum potential that humans have. Individuals within this level view rules, social norms, and power structures as an intrinsic part of reality and believe there is no way to change them. They do not recognize that they are seeing the world through a specific lens that biases their view.

Chapter 5

Going beyond mainstream

If you are trying to be normal, you do not know how amazing you can be. Never mind, amazing is too mainstream these days. Try being yourself, it is better than normal.

Anonymous

At the post-conventional tier (which represents approximately 18% of the population in Western nations), people realize that the meaning we make of things depends on our relative position regarding them, on our perspective and interpretation of them. Therefore, there is no absolute or objective reality.

People begin to move away from increased differentiation toward greater integration. They are more concerned with how we are connected to others rather than our differences, moving away from the individualistic perspective. They also start to question the critical assumptions of the previous stages, including the reality of the existence of a separate self. At the post-conventional stages, the world is taken as a dynamic and interconnected system rather than a random assortment of individual elements and events. Somehow, we start our life journey embedded with our mother, and we grow by gradually differentiating and discovering ourselves as independent and separate selves. Paradoxically, we reach the latest stages by getting closer and closer to becoming one with everything.

Since this book is primarily interested in exploring the latest stages of human development, we will specifically dedicate the next chapter to describing in depth the characteristics of people at this stage: Individualists, Strategists, Alchemists, and Unitives. But before that, let's try to answer some intriguing questions...

What makes us transition between stages? The reasons that cause people to move from one stage to the next are a mystery. Having a disorienting dilemma, or struggling with something we cannot understand from our current perspective, may lead to a later stage. Those dilemmas usually come disguised as a crisis: our partner passes away, we are diagnosed with a serious disease, we are fired, we lose faith... Often, the expansion that can come as a consequence of such a big shock is a horizontal one, with no change in developmental level or modification in our worldview. Thus, it just represents a deepening of the space we inhabit in the present.

How difficult is it to progress from one stage to the next? It is certainly not easy since inner development requires uncertainty and ambiguity, which most people try to avoid at all costs. Disequilibrium tends to create anxiety, and we tend to avoid experiences that can challenge us and steer clear of the information that may make us question our assumptions. We are interested in anything else besides growing up by being exposed to views that challenge our current perspective. We prefer to maintain stable self-perceptions, belief systems, and relationship patterns, even if we are dissatisfied and discontent. Unless life pushes us, we are not likely to overcome our limitations. We all tend to find comfortable niches that protect us from questioning.

People must develop to a higher level of complexity to move to the next stage. Even if they can cognitively understand a later stage than the one they are at, they look through their filter to interpret that last level. As we just noted, movement from one stage to the next seems to require some dissonance in life and is unrelated to age. We need to consider that simple change is not synonymous with structural development. The latter implies holding increased complexity, and once attained, it is not lost.

Even though the currently predominant conventional (Expert and Achiever) levels have created the current global technology, political systems, and science that have solved many crucial problems of humanity, these worldviews are also responsible for significant issues we are now facing on the planet. It is partly due to the limited, short-term, and empirical mode of reasoning. A method of thinking that is analytic and geared toward achieving planned goals is inadequate when dealing with essential matters. It is irrelevant when deciding which goals to aim at and when challenging some of the bases commonly taken for granted.

Adapting to our current complex global and local challenges can no longer be done with technical expertise, even with cutting-edge technology. Nor can it be solved by charismatic or determined leaders. Our postmodern society requires us to go beyond merely acquiring specific skills or mastering certain knowledge. What is needed is an apparent expansion of our consciousness beyond the conventional mindset, which is no longer well-equipped to respond effectively.

It is also impossible for anyone to make a lasting contribution to the world's welfare on a larger scale without first reaching a complete release from all selfish intent, all blind ego decisions, and all belief that crystallized views are correct. Especially when such statements are unduly conditioned by environment, background, culture, and a myopic perspective. We urgently need a consciousness shift on the planet. An awareness that our purpose cannot be fulfilled by accumulating material resources but instead by doing the greatest good. We must acknowledge that the concentration of wealth and the unwillingness to share is insane. It is, in fact, one of the main factors in creating the world's most persistent and striking social and political dilemmas we are facing now.

Moreover, we must accompany it with a solid motivation to seek and find peace. If everyone undertook this, we would end all wars, eliminate conflict, prevent injustice, and bring everlasting world peace. What is needed is not a change of circumstances, politics, or institutions but a change of consciousness. We have already tried the usual way, and observing our current time, it has not gotten us very far. We continuously encounter the same troubles without any stable solution that includes us all.

Earth has never been easy for creators, healers, or cutting-edge thought leaders. They seemed to be motivated by ideals for which the world was not ready. Those who did not fit in the box of the majority were typically met with much resistance. The less conventional they were, the more likelihood of being persecuted, condemned, and even killed. It has always been challenging to be different and more developed.

Cognitive development is necessary but not sufficient for consciousness development. Therefore, higher education and professional training do not guarantee movement into the post-conventional tier. Why are there so few people at these higher stages? Why does the development of these stages seem so challenging? It could be blamed on the lack of developmental opportunities and social support to keep progressing in our culture.

In Australia, for instance, there is a leadership program that tries to promote the advancement of participants toward the post-conventional tier. Those programs take executives to environments that they might otherwise never encounter. They serve meals in a homeless center; they work with people with disabilities to help them find a suitable job; they talk to prisoners about their living conditions; they sit with indigenous elders to discuss challenges in their communities; they go into farmers' fields, they sit on a murder or drug deal trial in a law court, they go to art performances, they visit business projects... And they are coached and guided to reflect upon all those new experiences and encounters. This way, they are exposed to other realities and learn that problems can be viewed through different glasses. They realize that issues cannot be considered in isolation, that we are all interrelated, that human nature is full of paradoxes, and that we filter reality through our habits, past experiences, and bias.

As guidelines, let's review some general common traits in the post-conventional tier:

- A rare willingness to accept the complexity and the ambiguity that comes into their lives.
- A high degree of introspection and inner awareness. They explore what is right for themselves and strive to express it.
- A search for an inner coherence between the person they currently are and what the environment demands, giving it much more importance than material gains or other conventional achievements such as financial success or professional accomplishments.
- Not necessarily an easy life, but they display positive emotional and mental skills and try to be free from regret, resentment, cynicism, hate, jealousy, and anger.
- A strong perception of their meaning in life arises from exploring who they are and their contribution to society.
- Many experience growth episodes with no external difficulty, but they choose instead to stay with an inner sense of discomfort and a lack of clarity. That is, they value growth for themselves.
- How one thinks is more important to them than what one believes. Worldview is thus seen as a self-constructed phenomenon.
- Cross-cultural experiences are helpful, as they present an opportunity to incorporate expanded knowledge and exposure in a personal and genuine experience.
- To them, growth becomes more significant than safety. Growth is taken as progress, learning, exploration, and deepening rather than staying stuck on the need for protection, preservation, conservation, or defending.

- As people increase their level of development, the inconsistencies that lead to growth do not come from the environment but from nonphysical transcendent sources.
- Somehow, they believe that Descartes got it wrong: our thoughts and emotions are an inevitable aspect of our being, but they can hide our inner depths from us too.
- When external hardship appears, conventional individuals tend to perceive the growth achieved as a change in behavior, whereas post-conventional individuals place greater emphasis on the increase in inner awareness.
- They demonstrate an exceptional sensitivity to their mental processes. They can show a clear-eyed admission of weakness and denial and even talk explicitly about automatic attempts to cope.
- When challenging experiences arrive, they admit their vulnerability, and rather than imposing quick meaning on those situations, they stay with it, keeping their heads above the waves. They allow themselves to be changed by those circumstances, for better or worse, simply by remaining actively engaged in and receptive to the experience.
- They can surrender, acknowledging that there are forces outside their control and beyond their intention.
- Peak experiences are vital at the beginning of the post-conventional tier, when the person first understands that consensual reality is just one version of an interpreted reality. However, as the growth continues, those experiences become less crucial and more natural.
- It is interesting to note that cultural dissonance is not a big deal for individuals at this tier. Once you consciously prioritize the inner experience and a more self-directed path, it becomes easier to leave the ordinary highway. Therefore, they normalize embracing beliefs that are not shared universally.

- They appreciate differences, whereas those in earlier stages look for similarity and stability.
- Tendency to increase their awareness through specific practices and activities such as meditation, various therapies, coaching, and yoga. Maintaining a committed spiritual practice that helps growth and increases inner awareness is seemingly universal, and it entails facing the strains that arise when perseverance is necessary.
- Although it would undoubtedly benefit Western societies, research has shown that post-conventional individuals are not drawn to social or political engagement in its current form.
- An increased inner awareness, self-exploration, and tolerance of ambiguity rather than seeking to master their environment.
- As the highest stages of post-conventional development are attained, people show a more remarkable ability to cope with uncertainty, accept responsibility for their choices, balance the needs of the self and those of others, and renounce the unattainable. For such individuals, interpersonal relations are intense and involve a recognition of the inevitable interdependence of all beings.

Chapter 6

Deciphering the highest

The greatest danger for most of us is not that our aim is too high and we miss it. Rather, it's that we aim too low, and we reach it.

Michelangelo

It can be fascinating to have a map of the highest stages of human development, providing a robust framework to understand that there is a new architecture of growth that we can consider and that will show us the way forward. It is a process that leads to more integration and transcendence, following movements in developmental psychology, values, worldview, and spirituality. We are not talking here about different states or even stages related to various phases of life. Knowing about the upper reaches of human development is crucial if we intend to continue our climb. It can accelerate our growth by creating connections and opening up unseen frontiers.

These are rungs on a ladder toward absolute unity, profound structural changes that we can go through, which become our new inner gravity center of thought processes and behavior. This is what we can all aspire to, in order to gain greater fulfillment, have an expansive contribution to the whole, and attain oneness.

We can now continue with the levels presented in chapter 4.

4. Individualists (around 15% of the adult population). People at this level of development realize that things are not necessarily what they seemed at earlier levels since the interpretation of reality always depends on the observer.

Their focus has shifted from achievement to psychological development and relationships, from purely rational analysis to a more holistic approach in which feelings and context are considered. Now the process becomes as interesting as the outcome. As they also realize that the way people make meaning of their lives is socially and culturally conditioned, scientific certainty as such starts breaking down, and they learn to examine their beliefs to test their assumptions as well. People at this stage have more tolerance of differences and alternative perspectives. Rather than accepting traditional ideas of the given, they understand that they are just interpretations of reality. Individualists move away from the notion that what is true is defined by culture and family. They can see the many conflicting aspects and polarities within themselves and the world, dealing with them in part by remaining in the moment and allowing life to be as it is. They now contemplate that all meaning depends upon the context and the relationships involved, but they have yet to figure out how to be responsible for this meaning-making.

Since old identities are no longer accepted without inquiry, Individualists seek unique personal accomplishments free of socially approved roles or endeavors. They often withdraw to some degree from external affairs or the daily tasks of organizations. Instead, they turn inward, searching for their unique talents, or they pursue their own burning questions. The desire for authenticity and integrity pushes them to let go of hypocrisies and phoniness usually present in their personality. They stop doing things simply because they think others expect them to. They stop living other people's designs for them. Those wishes that lock people into patterns of behavior—and are considered to be one's own—are now discovered to have been automatically accepted by one's society, family, and culture.

Since Individualists explore their feelings and motivations, they also become aware of how easily one can fool oneself. The possibility of defensive self-deception, bias, and distortion based on one's culture is now seen as a real danger.

They are interested in human rights and freeing humans from dogma, greed, and judgment. Equality is vital to them, for they do not prioritize any life over any other.

Because they are interested in spontaneity, freedom, and pursuing their paths, others (especially Achievers) may consider them unpredictable dreamers that do not accomplish much.

Feedback is viewed as an essential component of self-knowledge and a vital means of uncovering the hidden aspects of one's own behavior. They value the importance of seeing both sides of an argument or choosing both sides of a polar pair rather than just one. They recognize the relativity of all positions. They would instead not impose their interpretations on others and try to respect and understand them. Individual differences are celebrated and valued in a way that Achievers cannot understand. They value personal freedom and allow others to be who they are and want to be.

5. Strategists (only 3% of people arrive at this very mature perspective). People at this stage consciously commit to creating a meaningful life for themselves and others through self-actualization. They are focused on becoming the most one can be, guided by big-picture principles. They feel that they can write their story. They believe that life is a personal journey and that each person must find their way. There is a path that applies to everyone, and each person is responsible for themselves and their fulfillment; they must come to terms with the internal conflicts of being human in their own way. Personal growth and becoming the most one can be are the primary motivations at this stage. Their greatest fear is not fulfilling their potential or failing to adhere to the principles they value such as justice, tolerance, and the dignity of people.

For Strategists, their psychological wellbeing is paramount, as well as self-reflecting on how to come to terms with inner conflict and needs. The relativism of the previous stage (which might easily lead to cynicism and distrust) changes to interpersonal commitment and responsibility to create one's own meaning. This feeling of being in charge allows Strategists to rediscover, retain, and integrate aspects of themselves that were too confusing or threatening for the Individualists to acknowledge. They can understand and treat others according to their level of awareness because Strategists are the first to understand that different people are functioning from different levels. Still, the Strategist does not view all approaches as equal, developing preferences based on his or her values and experience.

Others are vital to one's wellbeing because they can provide wisdom and deeper self-knowledge through the exchange. Mutual interdependence is highly respected, and there is a sense of responsibility toward others. Wanting to help others grow is one of the main drives for Strategists. Psychologists, consultants, coaches, and therapists are often at this stage, and sometimes even executives and leaders have this inner impulse. When Strategists encounter resistance to their attempts to help others reach their full potential, they may become impatient with the other person's slow development or frustrated with the person's reluctance to grow. This is one of the flaws at this stage.

Feedback is essential to Strategists, even if they are pretty discriminating about what they receive, analyzing it and using what is helpful. They approach life as a learning experience and focus on their own development and the development of anyone important to them. They have an intense desire to grow, and inner authenticity is crucial for them. They can establish respectful boundaries with others while still connecting as colleagues in life.

Greater awareness of their inner depth also allows them to use dreams, metaphors, and imagination much more freely than people at earlier stages. They allow thoughts to fly, and vision is no longer contained by logical convention. Therefore, they are often intuitive, highly creative, outside-the-box thinkers. Strategists are also extremely self-reflective, constantly observing and reevaluating themselves, others, and the world.

Strategists often find the daily aspects of making a living a distraction from their real passions. However, their contributions can be impactful if their passion involves leading others or giving a form of service to others. They can become charismatic leaders, following their convictions regardless of personal consequences. If their convictions lead them in a direction helpful to others, the outcomes can be hugely positive.

They have no problem expressing their inner conflicts, ambiguity, and self-doubt or revealing elevated self-esteem. Although they experience role conflicts and dilemmas intensely, they recognize these are inevitable. Unlike people at the later stages, Strategists try very hard to keep their act together and appear reasonable, mature, and balanced.

They also have a solid motivation to improve through their effort and willpower and strong confidence in their ability to do so. That is probably why others can sometimes see them as arrogant and pushy. Strategists are often so strong-willed and focused that they will not stop their deliberate approach to growth until every practice they can learn has been deepened and exhausted. They do not contemplate that this is also coming from the ego, and it is necessary to let it go to move to later levels.

6. Alchemists (only 1% of the population arrive at this rare altitude). Individuals here begin to move away from an ego-based self-identity. They start to see how humans limit themselves with their mental maps. As they start shifting their identity to transpersonal awareness, the personality begins to question the assumption of the self as a genuinely independent, separate, and self-contained entity in an isolated, disconnected, and meaningless world. Boundaries start to dissolve as the personality moves to interdependence at all levels: body, mind, spirit, environment, others, and cosmos. So, they see themselves embedded in the totality of what it is. This expansion of perspective results from their increased openness, trusting one's emotions and intuitions. There is also a willingness to look at their life as part of a process and the world as a system of relationships and patterns of interaction. Rather than as individual ego-selves living in existential isolation, separated and independent of each other.

They become aware of the profound splits and paradoxes inherent to rational thought. They have one foot in the separate self and the other in the transcendent. Somehow, they experience the self partly from an independent and individual entity's perspective and partly as the infinite connected to the rest of the universe. Now, they can contemplate their ego for what it is (a map of reality, a way of seeing things) rather than something solid, but they have yet to transcend it entirely. Therefore, the separate self is no longer solidly authentic for them, but it is part of their experience of life as they begin to disidentify with it. That is part of them, but it is complemented by an infinite number of interconnections they share with the rest of the universe. It is not something they know about but rather something they feel.

At this stage, people seem to depart from the very literal adherence to a specific philosophy and practice that can be seen at earlier levels of development. Although Alchemists (and Unitives) can still be genuinely interested in their practices and studies with particular schools of thought or spiritual tradition, they do not have any rigid or unequivocal endorsement of any given group or worldview. Absolute and inflexible adherence to any single doctrine becomes an obstacle to further development.

They can put together and integrate different approaches, ideas, and concepts. They have an extraordinary ability to deal with complexity. While others may admire this talent, they cannot understand the fullness and complexity of this work. Few others are like them; therefore, there are few with whom they can share their experience and perspective on life. They have also deconstructed what so many others take as truth and reality, so all this can leave Alchemists feeling unseen, isolated, often misunderstood, and lonely.

Judgments and thoughts about anything outside the self are finally recognized as one's projections. Awareness of the mind and the emotions making up these feelings, stories, and judgments are closely related to one's own interior. It gets more patent that the common dualistic way of looking at the world fails to consider the arbitrary nature of all these divisions and that each pair of opposites arises together and they depend upon each other. Therefore, it becomes clearer that much human suffering stems from the divide between what we desperately want and pursue and what we dislike and attempt to escape.

Feedback can still be constructive, but it takes a new tone here. When one has developed the capacity to witness and knows that opinions and judgments are never objective but tainted by personal projections, what parts of the feedback should one take seriously? Sometimes cynicism and skepticism can arise, and they may not accept input well if they sense that there is no fundamental understanding of the complexity they are trying to bring forth.

They have a genuine desire for humility, for they know that they can understand some things that others cannot, and they know how the ego wants to take credit for this advanced comprehension.

At some point, they usually go through what the sixteenth-century Spanish mystic St. John of the Cross named "the dark night of the soul." This process generally emerges after a spiritual seeker has attained much spiritual growth. It has to do with realizing that the ego is an illusion and never really existed. The person feels stuck in the dark with no hope of seeing the light again. Since it is not mentioned that much in spiritual texts and teachings, and they have never gone through anything similar before, they feel very much alone and lost. Knowing this process is a natural step forward can be a great relief.

They eventually become more familiar with the silent witness, needing fewer tools to tame and empty the mind to find silence within. This witness becomes more activated during waking hours, and they continuously observe all the illusions played out in their daily lives. They also start to get ideas about how they might use those illusions and constructs as mechanisms for a better world.

Most people can immediately recognize them as having remarkable intelligence, though they may not be able to put their finger on their qualities immediately. They have a lot of compassion and general care for almost everyone, with an inexplicable way of speaking to nearly anyone and adapting to their level of understanding. They also have a highly developed ability to trust the process of whatever is going on.

They usually have high self-confidence that can seem arrogant to others. They are generally very confident in their choices and may even suggest that if someone cannot go along with their way of doing things, they should not participate. This can appear quite paradoxical to others, especially when they also perceive their great compassion and how they are willing to yield in so many kind ways, except in the personal areas of their giving of their perceived gifts to the world. Probably, this comes because they need to make these high-level choices.

Alchemists embrace post-material values and become oriented toward self-expression and authenticity. They tend to accept the inherent dilemmas of being human and the fact that life is impermanent and involves pain no matter what. This surrender is like that of a person with cancer who accepts their situation and becomes calm and peaceful, affecting those around them. For them, inner awareness alone is insufficient; it also needs to be expressed in one's being, integrated into one's actions and behavior, and indeed embodied in one's continuous presence in the world.

Since their life becomes an ongoing meditation, and they bring their complex understandings into the world intending to be of service, their spiritual practices are usually less about sitting in contemplation.

This is the first developmental level with a wide enough perspective to fully understand and empathize with the existential situation of those at previous levels. Therefore they can appreciate the strategies of others. This places them in an ideal position to be great mentors or coaches. Having a lower need for ego gratification and an ability to put feelings of self-importance aside, they are usually more effective in helping others than Strategists.

7. Unitives (scarce, less than 0.5% of the population). One of the main differences from the previous stage is that people evolve from a primarily cognitive-structural approach to an attentional-spiritual one. They can experience the humanness of individuals at all stages of awareness and become aware of the human essence they have in common. Therefore, they accept others as they are without trying to control them. They respect the essence of others and hence do not need them to be different from who they are.

They achieve a kind of consciousness in which everything is accepted without exception. They have let go of the idea that struggle will solve anything. Somehow, they can go to the essence, to what is beyond the bad and the good, the apparent opposites and duality. They have understood that it is not by pushing out what is not pleasant or is not aligned with their belief system that they are in harmony. They know you must change and heal yourself first, not change anyone or anything else. They understand that you can positively affect others when you increase your level of consciousness. The most significant responsibility is to love the world as it is and appreciate the beauty and value of everyone living here.

This is somehow the stage that most embodies the transcendental and the spiritual, experiencing themselves and others as part of ongoing humanity, fulfilling the destiny of evolution. They view life on Earth as a temporary and voluntary separation from Source, to which everyone will eventually return. Zen master Genpo Roshi said that the awakened person is "the one who chooses to be a human being."

People at this stage take peak experiences for granted, perhaps because they are readily available to them now. At previous developmental levels, people viewed them as extraordinary. And since they have such an openness and alignment to truth and beauty, having visionary experiences becomes another way of comprehending reality in addition to the rational mind. As Cook-Greuter states: "Doing or thinking are just modes of existing, but not intrinsically more valuable than feeling, being or non-being."

No matter how impressive their accomplishments may be, they see their insignificance in the grand scheme. At the same time, they are aware that their contribution (and everyone else's) to the universe is an essential part of the whole. They can accept everything and everyone as they are, without any need to change themselves or anyone else for that matter. They care about the plight of the human condition, show kindness to all, and embrace compassion. Their judgment and reasoning have developed to be guided by morality and loving-kindness. They can both contemplate the infinity of the universe and their friend needing a helpful hand at the same level. The rational mind is not seen as a limitation but rather as another form of being human, sometimes beneficial and at other times best kept out of the picture.

They can step out of the cyclone of the Alchemist's complex mind and sit in the eye of the typhoon even as it spins around them, letting go of the complexity even as they live within it. They root themselves in a place of peace, acceptance, and inner silence that permeates their lives. Thus, they respect their motivation to intervene in some cases and leave things alone in others.

All paradoxes are integrated here. Death and birth, joy and pain, are seen as natural patterns of the flux of life and to be noticed and experienced as they are. They have feelings of belonging and feelings of uniqueness without any tension. They can take multiple points of view and shift focus effortlessly among many states of awareness. The world is where all opposites are necessary and intertwined, instead of seeing life dualistically, where some things are desirable and others not. They are just ideas (subject to change) rather than intrinsic characteristics of things, events, or people. They can see perfection underlying every occasion and every situation since they can adopt a bigger-picture perspective.

The movement to enlightenment is a leap, not a step, and of a different magnitude altogether. Going from Alchemist to Unitive is a quantum leap in experience and outlook, and also discontinuous from the previous pattern of gradually being able to reframe and expand one's perspective.

Although they still have a sense of being a center of awareness in a body, they no longer experience themselves as separate. Unlike the previous stage, this is not just an idea they can intellectually grasp. It is also felt and experienced as such. This is an entirely new and different way of experiencing human existence and consciousness, with a more universal perspective. They can take on the witness's philosophy and approach things openly. It is sometimes referred to as pure consciousness, awareness without content. They perceive everything that enters their attention, but nothing is judged as better, worse, or more appropriate. There is a fluid, open-ended self-identity. Moreover, these individuals can integrate and use their transcendent experiences more often.

Other people tend to perceive Unitives as not sufficiently engaged in the goals, pursuits, and worries common to other human beings. However, they act as catalysts in shaping others' lives. By being the way they are, they challenge the perspective of others and serve as alternative examples of what a human being can become on Earth. Their capacity to take others as a whole, their tendency to interact in non-demanding ways, their humility, and their grace can have a subtle but profound effect on others.

As we can observe, the ego is no longer center stage here. Instead, it leaves room for a present feeling of gratitude, awe, and wonder for life, with a deep sense of universal connectedness, seeing the sacred in the ordinary. At this highest level, they give up the search for identity and become a witness to the process of self-becoming. They feel they have finally found what they were looking for. As the search is over, they inhabit an all-pervading peace and harmony at all times.

Unitives live fully in the now. Being in the present moment happens naturally because they are not focused on regrets or hurts from the past, nor are they longing for something better in the future.

Feedback is accepted readily where appropriate. There is lightness at this stage, without extremes of emotions. Since they have a low degree of identification with the separate self and tend to feel connected to humanity and the universe, it is natural for them to trust the way things are and where they are going without feeling any trace of resistance. Of course, they see that the world contains much suffering and problems. Nevertheless, addressing them (when appropriate) is just part of the universal dance. Here is where the Buddhist Bodhisattva vow is more pertinent and precise: the awakened being who commits himself to staying in the world until all beings have also been liberated. It is a transpersonal stage in which the "soul" is at peace.

Part III

Spirituality as the passport

Science is not only compatible with spirituality; it is a profound source of spirituality. When we recognize our place in an immensity of light-years and the passage of ages, when we grasp life's intricacy, beauty, and subtlety, then that soaring feeling, that sense of elation and humility combined, is surely spiritual. So are our emotions in the presence of great art or music or literature, or acts of exemplary selfless courage such as those of Mohandas Gandhi or Martin Luther King Jr. The notion that science and spirituality are somehow mutually exclusive does a disservice to both.

Carl Sagan

Chapter 7

Transcendence, or the spiritual dimension

Whatever your trials, remind yourself that you are a spirit and are capable of changing your destiny.

Omraam Mikhael Aivanhov

For too long, we have created institutions and roles in society that are artificial stratagems whose purpose was—and continues to be—to facilitate survival. We have identified with limited concepts that reduced us to feel like evolved animals, prisoners of our instincts, our aggressive impulses, our automatic compulsions, our crazy emotions that we could not manage, and our egotistic and selfish thoughts. All of which direct us to run away from the unpleasant and obtain more pleasure at any cost. We become too occupied with all these mechanisms to leave room for anything else.

Human development cannot be understood from a biological standpoint alone; genetic and environmental factors are not the only influences that shape the course of a person across their lifespan. Human beings are open to elements other than physical data alone. We must recognize consciousness's fundamental and foundational role as a key—but frequently overlooked— factor influencing our development. When we are in touch with the transpersonal or spiritual part of ourselves, there is a permanent sense of purpose. Deep down, we know that our experiences matter and that there is meaning in our lives— regardless of how it may be obscured by grief, doubt, anger, apathy, or frustration. Modern science has been an outstanding achievement for humankind. But now, we need to go beyond its narrow focus on logic, mathematics, and the mundane world to a broader science that includes other realms of consciousness, such as truths of the inner world.

Though personal memories are retained, and ongoing interpretations of circumstances through the self give us a unique sense of identity and continuity, the ego changes as we go through the various stages of development. Changes in the environment, circumstances, and personal situations are usually linked. However, the only absolute stability is the inner, transpersonal essence behind all physical body, mind, and personality constructions.

There comes a time when the soul has reached the furthermost point of its journey of separation and alienation and is ready to begin the journey of reunion and integration. Typically, the soul is gradually infused with inner discontent. This profound dissatisfaction cannot be filled with anything at hand and slowly filters into the consciousness of the human mind. Hopefully, that is when the person begins to turn inward, to domesticate the ego and its reactions, and search for a path to reconnect with Source, Divinity, Pure Consciousness, Godhead, Brahma, the Absolute, the Universal Spirit.

We have forgotten who we are: fragments of Source that have briefly incarnated as humans. It is only a question of time before everybody realizes that we are interrelated to all living creatures, as we are all emanations of the One and, therefore, intimately linked to each other. Our fundamental task is discovering that an expansive world lies ahead beyond the narrow restraints and loneliness of this limited disguise as *Homo sapiens*. Beyond the apparent boundaries of egocentric views exists a vast new dimension of reality with a cosmic highway that allows us to contribute to the universe's evolution. Life on Earth is but an ephemeral phase of existence. Our challenge now is to perceive it with our narrow and restricted senses and live accordingly—a task not for the fainthearted or the superficial.

The exercise of transcendence and spiritual transformation has become paramount in our time—because our technology has immense destructive power, which allows us to damage not just our neighbors but many others physically distant from us. By acting with a continuous lack of ethics, we are leaving an over-exploited Earth with reduced possibilities for healthy living, and we are sadly endangering our children's future. When our primary motivation is getting more for ourselves at any price, even if others will have to pay the cost of our material success, we will leave corpses behind. We must realize the interconnectedness of everything and even acknowledge our responsibility for what we think and feel, for what we say and do, to shift to a more harmonious way of living. Even though it is less obvious, psychological pollution is equally harmful. The negativity, fears, manipulation, conflicts, and rage we generate and emanate daily with our thoughts have similar destructive power to radioactive waste.

Technological development without an increase in consciousness will end up in human enslavement and destruction. Using it in an egocentric and selfish manner leads us to a profound social and planetary crisis. Artificial Intelligence and bioengineering make it possible to hack human beings, control human desire, and re-engineer feelings. Without transcendence, life is reduced to matter, and then we easily fall into apathy, separation, confrontation, nihilism, and alienation because we lose sight of our spiritual and cosmic origin. As we forget who we really are, we stay imprisoned in a narrow view of who we think we are, and we disconnect ourselves from our inner guidance and compassion for all living creatures at all levels.

The general materialistic, reductionist, and deterministic worldview has led to a perception of separateness and isolation from others. It justifies any means to achieve the interests of a powerful few. It artificially creates confrontation that ends up in absurd wars. Not only that, but it imposes laws to protect just the rights of the ruling elite. It curtails people's freedom. It installs institutions that take money from the poor to enrich the billionaires. We can see its numerous destructive effects on an individual and a global scale, making this planet quite tricky. We will contribute to the destruction of the human race and Mother Earth if we do not modify our understanding of life and reality into something more holistic that integrates everyone.

We may have to transcend the old mechanistic and deterministic Newtonian paradigm that presupposes that the objective and subjective worlds are entirely independent. In other words, it states that a scientist can be objective, and his intellectual work does not project his view on his theories, models, and objects of study. We may need to fully embrace the new paradigm of quantum physics and integral science, which states that the mind and consciousness are not independent of the physical world. On the contrary, they make up its basic structure. According to this perspective, we are active participants worldwide, so we cannot separate ourselves from the observed. In other words, we constantly affect physical systems. We are not separated from the external world; we are embedded in it; there is no real distinction between in and out. Besides, we know now that our human body is just a misleading assemblage of empty spaces on an empty planet in an empty universe. Everything is 99.9999% space, which deeply questions our notions of existence at its core.

The objective reality is not as independent of us as we believe, and we are not isolated from each other. Experiments have been carried out trying to measure the position and speed of one particle (something impossible according to Heisenberg's principle of uncertainty because observing modifies the observed). Scientists were able to measure the position of two particles split—after perceiving how they moved at the same speed in opposite directions. The first study took place at the

University of Geneva and was carried out twice. In 1998, the nonlocal entanglement of both photons was demonstrated over 11 kilometers of optical fiber. In 2004, the experiment was repeated, and the result showed a connection over 50 kilometers. Another proof of what Eastern philosophies have known for hundreds of years: we are all interconnected.

What is self-transcendence? It is a state of Unitive consciousness where the individual self is not that present because there is no clear distinction between self and other. The person is simply aware of being a constituent of the evolution of the cosmos. This Unitive perspective may be described as a spiritual fusion with nature and its source. The researcher Robert Cloninger says: "The person may identify (or feel a sense of spiritual union) with anything and everything. They may experience the feeling that they are part of or being guided by a wonderful intelligence, which is possibly the divine source of all phenomena."

Mystics of all ages and places have been able to transcend the different conceptual schemes provided by their culture, language, and dogmas and consequently access a direct intuitive understanding of reality. The mystical experience is universal and timeless, while its interpretation is culturally and historically determined. Therefore, the experience of transcendence is identical for all. It would be interpreted as emptiness or *sunyata* by a Mahayana Buddhist, as Brahman by an Advaita Vedantin, as the union with God by a Christian, or as an objectless absorption by a practitioner of Patanjali's yoga. Only the interpretation differs.

There is a primordial truth where all contemplative traditions converge: the existence of an absolute and pure Consciousness, Universal mind, or Source that constitutes the fundamental essence of both human nature and the totality of reality. That is a simultaneously immanent and all-pervading Spirit that is fundamentally present in human consciousness.

This spirit forms the ultimate referent for what can be regarded as real, authentic, valuable, everlasting, and pure. The quantum physicist John Hagelin also explains the primary reality of consciousness. Based on the superstring theory, the unified field theory affirms that a single and universal unified field is the basis of all natural forms and phenomena.

When our rationality does not filter out what we can apprehend, our mind can access a broad band of information well beyond the information available through our five sensory organs. That is why mystical practices, such as meditation, are best suited to processes of de-automatization or deconditioning of socially and culturally learned concepts and cognitive structures through which we usually apprehend ourselves and the world. They become direct highways to transcendence without the mediation of beliefs, expectations, and rationalization that tend to build walls between the Absolute and us. As in many other traditions, in the Hindu Upanishads, it is highlighted that "Thou art that," that is, the essential unity between the individual soul and the divine.

Chapter 8

Spiritual experiences

Can you describe music to someone using only words?

Can you describe the emotion of love only using the symbols of words?

Words are only effective at communicating experience if the experience is already known. You know color, music, and emotion because you have perceived them directly.

Enlightenment is not an experience that one already has a reference for, and so a word description is not likely to be meaningful enough to convey an understanding.

Gary van Warmerdam

First, we should make a distinction between spirituality and religion. Religion conceptualizes formalized behaviors such as prayers and rituals, beliefs and dogmas associated with distinct faith traditions. Conversely, spirituality can be defined as the emotional connection people experience with whatever they consider divine or sacred. It could be one God for some, multiple divinities for others, emptiness for Buddhists, or nature for atheists.

In most spiritual lineages, preliminary practices relate to concrete ethical actions and delaying the gratification of the senses and instinctual impulses. For example, in Theravada and Tibetan Buddhism, Hinduism, and Orthodox Christianity, the preliminary ethics practices are the first stages of spiritual practice, following explicit rules. Entire paths are built around these precise teachings and are critical to forming a robust base upon which more advanced and subtle spiritual practices are constructed.

Every human being is born with inner ideals and spiritual values that seek fulfillment, and the seed remains in each person to potentially try to actualize those ideals and values. Negative expectations or beliefs, fears, prejudices, and doubts can diminish the person's openness and awareness of her natural impulses toward spiritual development, which Abraham Maslow called "the farther reaches of human development."

Mainstream psychology considers exceptional human experiences anomalous (or out of the norm) because of the already-established standardized divisions. Their commitment to a materialistic, reductionist, and mechanical view of nature makes it very hard to understand authentic mysticism based on spiritual experiences. The separation between what is thought normal and what is not is based on fixed ideas and beliefs. It causes a fight between what is believed to be intelligent, rational, and realistic on the one hand and crazy, irrational, and unrealistic—if not completely stupid—on the other. Therefore, concepts such as highest or ultimate potential, transcendence, or spirit are seen as a threat to the scientific legitimacy of psychology. In fact, in our current society, areas outside the boundaries of the laboratory are off-limits and taboo subjects. All too often, what cannot be proven in the laboratory is presumed not to exist. If we filter reality with narrow physical nets, it will be almost impossible to catch the vast realm of consciousness.

However, transpersonal psychology is more open-minded and considers exceptional human experiences extensions of ordinary creativity. The rarity and usualness of a phenomenon do not automatically detract from its legitimacy or significance. Transpersonal experiences are usually interpreted as spiritual and can occur spontaneously or through meditation, prayer, being in connection with nature, sexuality, and other situations. They include peak or inspirational experiences in which the universe is perceived as peaceful, harmonious, and unified. There is no need to put aside the reasoning mind. The idea is to expand the conscious mind by opening the focus to alternative modes of perception. Thus, we can view reality in a more expanded manner, gaining a more precise panorama of the nature of reality and a greater awareness of events, their meaning, and the interconnectedness we were previously unaware of.

Why are these kinds of experiences so rare? Considering how difficult it is to be present and to explore the depths of your psyche, it is even harder to explore the greater dimensions of one's self and open up the gate to exceptional and transformative capacities. Even if you are intellectually aware of it, this is not enough to be acquainted with the practical side of it.

All too often, people become inundated by the contamination of trivialities of everyday existence. Thus, finding more profound meaning in their lives comes through transforming and spiritual experiences in which they become actively involved, and this puts them in touch with the purpose of life. What is frequently required to consciously rise to states of spiritual advancement in a person's life is a belief in their existence and a disciplined work that allows their emergence and accessibility. More specifically, engaging in a spiritual practice seriously and for a sufficient amount of time to start opening the doors that appear closed (or nonexistent) to the average person. Frequently, disciplined spiritual practice is required to open that gate that appears locked and reveal what is hidden to the untrained eye. When done for a sufficient time, it can generate enough experiential data to counteract our limited ideas about reality. This way, it becomes easier for the egotistically oriented parts of ourselves to accept the existence of other streams of perception and consciousness. Only then can the person's ideas of reality be affected and changed by a more comprehensive understanding given through personal experience. To accomplish that, the individual has to accept that within the human psyche there exists an inherent self-transcending principle that impels the person toward what Plato called "the True, the Good, and the Beautiful."

One element critical in spiritual advancement is the expansion of awareness. In the first stages, it begins and ends with one's skin. It gradually moves to recognize others and includes one's community. In the latest stages, one does not see any essential difference between oneself and all sentient beings.

At the beginning of our process of inner evolution, the person is only aware of the concrete: how one looks, how others look, the food one takes, the rules one follows, and so on. Later, the person becomes aware of his thought processes, his emotions as they arise, the needs of others... If the personal progress continues, his awareness becomes more refined as he is able to notice more subtleties. For example, energetic connections, the inner voice of guidance, seeing one's projections onto others, and following the focus of one's awareness in the present with openness, without the need to analyze it.

Spiritual experiences are challenging to describe in words. Pure knowing and pure feeling are often called ineffable because they occur without the necessity for symbols or comments that would aid in their interpretation and communication to others. As awareness becomes less physically oriented, the need for mental representations falls away, being just illustrations of the original experience. In Buddhism, such experiences of consciousness without symbols are interpreted as states of emptiness. We are so language-oriented that when form and words vanish, we deduce that being itself also disappears. Since spiritual states such as mysticism are relatively rare and difficult to translate to verbally structured thought, symbols and metaphors generally convey mystic inner realizations that cannot be perceived by ordinary physically oriented consciousness.

Transcendental experiences are direct ways of knowing where your awareness is suddenly expanded with no apparent limits, which the rational mind cannot comprehend. We are not always prepared for those situations; occasionally, they throw you out of balance and make you question your sanity. As the mystical saint St. John of the Cross wrote, "When the divine light of contemplation assails the soul that is not wholly enlightened, it causes spiritual darkness within it." Gradually, you can integrate them as natural occurrences and as alternative ways of apprehending reality with its multiple layers and subtleties on the path of awakening.

Mystical experiences involve a suspension of conventional perception (which often happens involuntarily and suddenly), usually last for a short time, and leave a rapturous afterglow that eventually drops away. Some of these experiences are characterized by feelings of purification and renewal: life and the world get transformed by a deep sense of loving-kindness to all. Some bring new knowledge because of communication from someone or somewhere else, and others present feelings of unity with God, nature, or the universe.

We must be careful because these experiences do not necessarily reveal a clear understanding of "me" as a construct in mind invested with a sense of self. On the contrary, they may even support inflation and narcissism as the ego takes ownership of them. The person believes that going through such occurrences makes you unique and superior.

All the main spiritual traditions assert that we live in a world hypnotized by our habitual social and cultural conditioning. Our normal state of consciousness is clouded, deluded, dreamlike, and somehow entranced—sleepwalkers running on automatic. Like in the movie *The Matrix*, we may think we are awake, yet we are actually asleep. Even if most people are entirely unaware of it. Thus, whether we know it or not, without mental training, we are prisoners of our minds. We are profoundly and unwittingly ensnared by a continuous inner dialogue and fantasy, which creates a pervasive illusion or distortion of reality (often called *maya* or *samsara*). Researchers Walsh and Shapiro state: "This condition is said to go unrecognized until we begin to subject our perceptual-cognitive process to rigorous scrutiny such as meditation." We must free our intellect from concepts taught to be true to wake up.

Higher intuitions and inspirations are usually received through contact with our transpersonal self, whether artistic, philosophical, scientific, ethical, or spiritual. Such connections typically come in the form of peak experiences that reveal to the individual part of his identity that lies beyond time and space and provide a bridge to other visions related to the greater self. These experiences are personal and irrefutable proof for the individual of an expansive world beyond the physical and the theoretical that, even if not thoroughly understood, changes something at the very core of the person. It opens a wide window surpassing personal roles, beliefs, physical time, separation, scarcity mindset, need for control, suffering, and limited personality. And even if the person returns to "normal" reality, its effects are never forgotten.

One of the most impactful spiritual experiences that cause transformative effects in some people is near-death experiences (NDEs). The conventional indicator of death is the cessation of electrophysiological activity in the brain. As medical technology has advanced, the opportunity has increased to intervene in the dying process and the capacity to bring individuals back to life. Consequently, the number of reported cases of near-death episodes has risen. The most exciting part is their transformative influence on the person's life afterward. Most people that go through this acknowledge a newfound capacity for joy in living that does not come from any religious belief. They lose any trace of fear of death. A shift in consciousness occurs whereby life in each moment becomes so vivid and rich that anxiety about future survival, whether in the body or out of it, ceases to be relevant.

The NDE is a passing event, but in many instances, it leaves a permanent trace, providing the person with a state of mystical consciousness, pretty stable, full of calmness and inner peace. Preoccupation with the future is no longer a focus, and personal needs become more personal preferences, regarded with more detachment than before. There is such a pervading sense of gratitude and awe, and what used to be perceived as unpleasant or depressive is now found to be beautiful and exciting.

After being nearly poisoned to death in Thailand during an attempted robbery, scientist John Wren-Lewis underwent a near-death experience that profoundly changed his worldview. He considered afterward that—contrary to what we usually believe—we have some hyperdefensive, hyperactive survival mechanism that is operative during the trance of so-called ordinary waking consciousness. This somehow blocks and shuts out of awareness the universal mystical consciousness characteristics of NDEs (and other transpersonal experiences), which are already the basis of our very existence. He wrote: "A close encounter with death can break this whole spell because the survival mechanism gives up at this point." Our challenge is to lift the veil of unconsciousness imposed by our endless daily tasks, automatic drives, and survival obsessions. It is the only way to reach higher levels of consciousness without approaching death's door.

A typical peak experience for parents is the birth of a baby. Watching this innocent little creature coming out of the mother's body, entrusting itself to the world, so beautiful and vulnerable, opens a deep sense of awe in almost anyone. This sacred moment opens parents' consciousness and makes them consciously or unconsciously in touch with their inner divinity, making them feel unconditional love and oneness. For a while, they can sense who they really are beyond the illusions. Unfortunately, this is usually just a temporary state of fulfillment. After a short time, things tend to settle down and get back to normal. Their opportunity for real awakening gets lost, and they adapt again to their habitual patterns of thinking and feeling. They will later recall that time as the happiest of their life, but they are unaware of the actual reasons for their feelings of bliss.

Another kind of transcendental experience has occurred to some astronauts when seeing the earth both from space and in space. Only around 500 astronauts have ever witnessed this direct view. For some, such a profound and life-changing experience shifted their whole perspective. Dr. Edgar Mitchell became the sixth man to walk on the moon. On the return trip to Earth, he had a mystical experience that changed his direction. He retired shortly after that from NASA and founded the Institute of Noetic Sciences to sponsor research into the nature of consciousness. Gazing through 240,000 miles (386,242.56 km) of space toward the stars and Earth, he suddenly experienced the universe as intelligent, loving, and harmonious. He conveyed it with the following words: "It was such a powerful experience. I suddenly realized that the molecules in my body, and the molecules in the spacecraft and my partners, had been prototyped, maybe even manufactured, in some ancient generation of stars. But instead of being an intellectual experience, it was a personal feeling... And that was accompanied by a sense of joy and ecstasy, which caused me to say: 'What is this?' It was only after I came back that I researched and found that the term in ancient Sanskrit was Samadhi."

It appears that everybody who goes to space is somehow touched by it; to some, it is an experience of being overwhelmed with awe and feeling blessed and connected. Nuclear physicist and founder of the World Space Center David Beaver puts it this way:

As you go into your mind in a contemplative way, the sense of the living reality of the planet becomes obvious. You become more aligned with the natural world. This is very akin to the direct perception of the astronauts, so it is no wonder that many people have likened the overview effect to a spiritual or meditative experience.

And as such, this sort of experience is available to all of us.

Another well-known example is Jill Bolte Taylor, a Harvard neuroscientist who went through what she calls a nirvana state while having a stroke. As she recounts it in her memoir, *A Stroke of Insight*, and in the many interviews she has given, in 1996 Dr. Taylor woke up in her apartment in Boston with a piercing pain behind her eye. A blood vessel in her brain had popped. Within minutes, her left hemisphere—the source of ego, analysis, judgment, and planning—began to fail her. The perpetual inner dialogue that typically fills our minds also disappeared, and her everyday perceptions were transformed. She shifted into the right hemisphere—the metaphorical, creative, intuitive, nonverbal, and emotional—at that moment. She began to notice that the atoms and molecules making up her body blended with the surrounding space. The whole world and the creatures in it were all part of the same magnificent shimmering energy. Her physical boundaries were no longer limited to her skin. After experiencing intense pain, she described how her body disconnected from her mind. "The energy of my spirit seemed to flow like a great whale gliding through a sea of silent euphoria." Paradoxically, while her spirit flew, her body struggled to survive. She had a clot the size of a golf ball in her head. Her left hemisphere was seriously damaged, so she lost essential analytical functions like speaking, understanding numbers or letters, and even recognizing her mother for a while.

Although her story is not typical of stroke victims, her left-brain injuries led her to a blissful spiritual experience. Surgery and eight years of recovery followed, but the impact of such an experience never left her. She states that every person "can step into the consciousness of [their] right hemisphere on command and be one with all that is." With a background as a brain scientist (she has a Ph.D. in life sciences with a specialty in neuroanatomy), she explains an event typically ethereal and pretty abstract with the language of science. The two hemispheres of the brain have highly diverse functions. Generally, the left brain gives us reasoning, ego, time, and logic. The right brain gives us creativity, intuition, empathy, connection, and so on. And we can all choose to live a more peaceful and spiritual life by sidestepping our left brain from time to time. This has nothing to do with religion, as she considers that "religion is a story that the left brain tells the right brain."

However, she confirms by her experience what spiritual seekers and meditation practitioners have always known, that a state of joy, harmony, and fulfillment is attainable right now, claiming that the left brain can be tamed and that "the more time we spend choosing to run the deep inner peace circuitry of our right hemispheres, the more peace we will project into the world, and the more peaceful our planet will be." Nothing else to add.

Chapter 9

Spiritual intelligence

What we see is not nature, but nature exposed to our method of questioning.

Werner Heisenberg

There appears to be a difference between spirituality and spiritual intelligence. Spirituality may be described as ultimate belonging or connection to the transcendental ground of being. Some define spirituality in terms of their relationship to God, fellow humans, or the earth. Others define it in terms of devotion and commitment to a particular faith or form of practice. It can also be described as the knowledge of yourself as a spirit or soul and the understanding of your highest spiritual qualities and attributes: love, peace, and bliss. Spirituality refers to the search for the sacred, ultimate meaning, higher consciousness, and transcendence.

Spiritual intelligence involves applying and embodying spiritual values and virtues to enhance daily life, wellbeing, and contribution to society. That is the expression of these innate qualities through thoughts, attitudes, and behaviors. Spiritual intelligence concerns the inner life of mind and spirit and its relationship to being and acting in the world. Spiritual intelligence implies a capacity for a profound understanding of existential questions and insight into multiple levels of consciousness. It is also related to deep self-expression and striving to find meaning in life as one's primary motivational forces. It also mobilizes the qualities and abilities of the soul through wisdom, compassion, integrity, joie de vivre, love, peace, harmony, equilibrium, and inner silence.

Spiritually intelligent individuals think and act with compassion and wisdom and can maintain inner peace and equanimity regardless of changing circumstances. Compassion is the most elevated stage of the development of emotional intelligence (heart), and wisdom is the most elevated stage of the intellect (head). The two wings are necessary to fly to the higher self or divinity. Inner peace and equanimity help the person maintain a healthy detachment to outcomes, not being carried away distressed by the suffering and injustice so present in our world, while being able to act with conviction and determination. A person with high spiritual intelligence may appear angry with others but remains calm due to his peaceful mind.

We can achieve satisfaction when we fully engage in the now and savor life. This is because existence is a moment in time, and we can fully experience each moment. One of the main parts of spiritual intelligence is the ability to treat everyday things, events, and relationships as if they were sacred. It is when we keep the awareness of the constant communion that essentially exists between the self and the world.

Viktor Frankl's view of the human condition clarified the difference between biologically rooted drives that push us and spiritually rooted yearnings that pull us. When the will to meaning is frustrated, the person experiences some existential frustration. When that happens, the life energy is projected into a lower dimension, becoming a craving for power. Or even lower, to an extent where the main obsession is the craving for pleasure. Without a sense of meaning beyond oneself, all these dimensions are experienced as neuroses and cause many of today's problems. Pleasure cannot be an end in itself but is rather a by-product of having done something meaningful. Likewise, power should be a means to care for more and have a broader positive influence. Only by transcending the narrow limits of self-interest by accepting a spiritual perspective can we liberate ourselves from self-serving attachments and constricted identifications.

Howard Gardner's pioneer work at Harvard on multiple intelligences has helped people understand that intelligence has different facets. His research has indicated that distinct kinds of intelligence develop relatively independently, and proficiency in one does not imply the same in another. Daniel Goleman's research on emotional intelligence showed that success in most areas depends on cognitive and emotional capacities. Ideally, spiritual intelligence would enable us to see things as they are, free from filters and unconscious distortions. In contrast to wishful thinking, attaching to dogmas, or grasping for certainty, exercising spiritual intelligence implies facing existential realities such as justice, suffering, altruism, and death and continuing the perennial search for meaning.

Nowadays, people from many traditions tend to view spirituality as being experiential rather than conceptual and transrational. Humans have three distinct forms of knowing: emotional, rational, and contemplative. These three ways are an integral part of spiritual intelligence.

Rational intelligence manages facts and information, using logic and analysis to make decisions. Emotional intelligence is necessary to understand and control one's emotions and feelings, and it entails listening, communicating, accepting feedback, and empathizing with different points of view. While a person's intelligence can be measured by how well they can solve problems, their emotional intelligence can be measured by how they behave. Emotional intelligence is not well-suited for solving technical or neutral issues or planning and executing tasks. Still, it can help evaluate proposed solutions from a global perspective. It is also the one that is capable of understanding and resolving social and personal issues to achieve the most significant benefit. We need both. Sound reasoning and intelligence present factual solutions to problems, but if we do not develop emotional intelligence, we may accept harmful approaches, solutions at any cost, or only superficially reliable improvements that bring damaging consequences.

Spiritual intelligence skills depend upon a certain amount of empathy and emotional awareness. It also requires the growth of cognitive complexity (since it confronts mystery and paradox). But if we wish to reach the highest stages of development, we must realize that rational and emotional intelligence are necessary but insufficient. Most of us have learned to be motivated by external factors, while a few have discovered that the deepest motivators are intrinsic. We can use our thoughts and will to inspire us. Nevertheless, a clear sense of meaning and purpose is the most profound motivator for any human being. This can only arise when we investigate and discover who we really are and where we are going at the deepest level. This is where emotional intelligence flows into spiritual intelligence. To understand the true meaning of events and perceive our purpose in this lifetime, we must first attain a state of self-awareness.

Here, contemplative practices such as meditation, yoga, prayer, or observation of the natural world are particularly relevant for polishing spiritual intelligence. This helps us tap into accurate insights and observe with mindfulness and awareness. Contemplation is knowledge that is neither conceptual nor emotional. It is an experiential mode of learning and self-knowledge. It exists within each of us but is covered over by discursive thinking and various emotions. Contemplative practices help us develop capacities for quieting the mind and concentrating intensely, even in the middle of distraction and action, which is characteristic of modern life. We need a calm, centered state to explore our purpose, behavior, and values. Silence is required to feel the presence of a transcendental dimension in life.

Spiritual development requires an ongoing dis-identification with the ego and integration of a personality. We must always be willing to adjust to circumstances, be open to the present moment, and be in touch with our inner depths. We must also be aware of our unity with everyone else and view everyone, including ourselves, with compassion. This refinement of the spirit is indicated by its ability to revere high values. And for it to be genuinely spiritual intelligence, it cannot be a momentary experience or even a state but must be a way of being and a way of life. It is impossible when it has not been integrated into the personality.

Spiritual intelligence comes from intellectual and emotional intelligence in the state of presence. The essential nature of this presence is shifting from ego to spirit. The closer we transcend our ego and become one with ultimate reality, the more powerful our presence will be. We inhabit the body as a temporary physical vehicle when we do that. We emanate peace, live in inner stillness, and feel a flow of fulfillment regardless of external changing circumstances and the number of challenges we may face. And this is something others can also perceive. Author and spiritual teacher Paul Brunton became aware of this when he visited the ashram of the great sage Ramana Maharishi in the 1930s. He wrote about his experiences when sitting close to him. How he was bathed in ineffable tranquility and bliss, radiation from this mysterious and imperturbable man who by all accounts was enlightened. The filmmaker and spiritual teacher Arnaud Desjardins also discussed similar experiences of in-depth transformation with his guru, Swami Prajnanpad (a university professor who became a Hindu monk). When these individuals enter a room, they fill it up with their light and calm presence, even if they do not speak.

Their energy, aura, and being benefit others in ways we cannot apprehend. Thus, others are touched by it. I have heard of many people who have also experienced this with the Dalai

Lama. Eminent psychologist Paul Ekman writes openly about his encounter with him in his book *Emotional Awareness* and how intensely he was impacted by it, even if he had no previous reverence or expectations. I can confirm it myself. Time after time, I was moved, recharged, and inspired by the Dalai Lama's presence, irrespective of the continent or the space where he was teaching.

Therefore, to the highest degree, spiritual intelligence is not about soft and fluffy feelings. It is deep compassion manifested in wise action. It demonstrates a profound personal integrity that aligns purpose and values, intending to serve humanity, always focused on the best outcomes and the big picture, ready to encourage and inspire others, serene even when the tide gets rough, and not triggered by egoistic reactions or egocentric desires. This is achievable immediately and will have a powerful, positive impact on humanity.

Chapter 10

Spiritual bypass

When we are spiritually healthy, we realize that we exist beyond the physical and our life has a sense of meaning and purpose.

Robyn L. Gobin

In 1984, psychologist and meditation teacher John Welwood came up with this term: "spiritual bypass." It refers to using spiritual practices and beliefs to avoid dealing with painful feelings, unhealed wounds, unresolved relationship issues, and developmental needs. It is a convenient manner of jumping directly to divinity without the hassle of struggling with uncomfortable aspects of life and ourselves. Furthermore, it is indeed a great temptation nowadays when being able to lead a "normal" life has become increasingly tricky and elusive: people find it harder and harder to earn a living with a meaningful job, to keep a long-term intimate relationship, to belong to and have the support of a community... Therefore, it is easier to sidestep the personal and the emotional troubles when you struggle to adapt and function in modern society by using spirituality to cover up what you cannot deal with.

Part of this is that we tend not to be inclined to face and work through our pain, choosing pain-numbing alternatives instead, regardless of how much suffering those seeming solutions can bring. Because this preference has deeply and thoroughly penetrated our culture, it has become the norm. Thus, spiritual bypassing reflects our collective habit of turning away from what is painful, escaping it, and believing it has no side effects. In spirituality, it is a usual strategy for avoiding pain and validating such avoidance, excusing it very convincingly. The spiritual impoverishment of contemporary society and the number of children raised without a nurturing and supportive family is growing. Divorce, traumatic circumstances, and lack of real support with children can all bring forth people who lack an inner sense of security and wellbeing. Those children grow up to become adults but still feel like impoverished kids. Their pain and sense of deficiency are reinforced by the isolation and denial of feelings that are so common in our culture. Many people seek a spiritual path, carrying this heavy burden upon their shoulders, what some psychologists call a "weak sense of self" or a "needy ego," with significant holes in their psyche and heart. This damaged sense of self is carried for years by harmful habits and bodily tensions, reinforced by the stories we keep telling ourselves and the mental images we fabricate.

Suppose we have a poor sense of self and continuously negate ourselves. In that case, it is natural to confuse inner impoverishment with selflessness and convince ourselves that distancing from it is the detachment some traditions advise. This only leads to passivity, which is related to indifference. Not conducive to awakening. This misperception can reinforce our underlying depression, frustration, and fear of the world, justifying our inability to find beauty, meaning, and the thrust to fully participate in life.

Spiritual bypassing is a persistent shadow of spirituality, manifesting in many ways, often without being acknowledged. Aspects of spiritual bypassing include emotional numbing and repression; overemphasis on the positive; blindness to anger; excessive detachment; taking weaknesses as compassion; incapacity to establish boundaries; focus only on cognitive skills with insufficient development of emotional intelligence; rejecting one's shadow elements; devaluation of the personal relative to the spiritual. We could also include delusions of having reached a high level of development, presenting oneself as a more realized or holy person, what Chögyam Trungpa called "spiritual materialism." In other words, becoming overly self-important or conceited. It can turn spirituality into a defense mechanism that lets us deny any negative aspects of ourselves or our behavior and stops us from trying to improve them.

This shortcut causes us to withdraw from ourselves and others, hiding behind a spiritual veil of metaphysical beliefs and practices. As author Robert Augustus Masters writes, it not only "distances us from our pain and difficult personal issues, but also our own authentic spirituality, stranding us in a metaphysical limbo, a zone of exaggerated gentleness, niceness, and superficiality." Trying to force a mood of equanimity in pleasure and pain only puts unnecessary stress on the mind, making the person dull, artificial, and tense. It is a mistake to copy the behavior of a realized master while remaining in the unrealized state. A person who appears to exhibit post-conventional morality may simply be repeating statements from others. How a person thinks, perceives reality, and acts in the world must be aligned.

It is a much subtler defense mechanism to detect than alcoholism, although any forms of psychological repression tend to be hard to identify and intervene. Spiritual bypassing is even more difficult to notice because it shows up as wisdom and evolution. You can always resort to meditation to disconnect and find some calmness when you have a conflict with your partner that has to be dealt with. Alternatively, you can distract yourself with the Internet when you need to get your act together and look for a job, or you can read a spiritual book or browse social media instead of feeling the pain of a broken dream.

It is one thing to understand things intellectually and another to completely overcome the emotional defenses we have built up to protect ourselves from vulnerability. If taking a spiritual path serves us to keep avoiding deeper issues, then our development will be arrested at some point. As Carl Jung said, "The personal unconscious must always be dealt with first... otherwise the gateway to the cosmic unconscious cannot be opened."

One of the shortcuts I have also often noticed is the rational bypass. It is a tendency to seek shelter in the mind, to live in and through thoughts alone. Also, to over-intellectualize and rationalize every situation, feeling, and behavior to escape the moment and unpleasant emotions. Head-tripping is usually a way to cut ourselves off from the area of feeling. I have seen it expressed as a profound capacity to articulate complex and interesting theories without delving into the heart of the matter or experiencing difficult circumstances. I have treated people with a high IQ and the ability to understand complexity rationally but who are complete failures in their personal lives.

It is too easy to do spiritual bypassing, using spiritual and esoteric concepts to sidestep real psychological work. You do it when you consider that you have already conquered high peaks of evolution, not realizing that you are lying to yourself about your development, intellectualizing principles and not embodying them. Even more in our times, with the proliferation of materialistic and simplistic self-help books, we can easily avoid addressing deeper issues and engage in a perpetual cycle of self-deception.

Certain practitioners get hooked on the idea of the ultimate truth. They believe that, since everything is perfect at a cosmic level, it is a sign of weakness to grieve at the separation from someone you love or to commit to a relationship. Instead of exploring and discussing how they feel, they shrug it off, saying, "But it is all emptiness." Absolutely! Our experience is never lasting; it is just that, experience. But this does not mean we cannot feel hurt or experience disappointment, for instance. Indeed, everything is ultimately impermanent, and the most painful emotions will come and go, changing in nature, intensity, and form.

However, knowing theoretically that things are ephemeral will not push us into awakening. This can only be done through experience. Allowing ourselves to feel it first, responding with compassion, and healing whatever is required without looking elsewhere while we try to convince ourselves that this is what wise and spiritual people do. Establishing ourselves on a higher plateau, pretending that we are above all feebleness, does not make sense. Adopting behaviors of spiritual masters without reaching that level of development tends to be widespread in certain circles. Imposing on oneself higher truths that lie beyond one's current existential condition without having integrated them first is a joke. Trying to live up to spiritual ideals, and denying our true feelings, cuts us off from an authentic path. We should not use spiritual teachings as an excuse for a defensive posture.

Spiritual practices such as meditation allow us to let go of the fixations of surface thoughts by not reacting to them automatically. It is not meant to be used as a bridge over troubled waters. We need some psychological work to open up the core of ourselves and clean it out before we can relate to our essence more directly. We have to be ourselves before we can let go of ourselves entirely. We have to be somebody before realizing that we are nobody. We must fully inhabit our bodies and wounds before discovering that we are none of them. We have to analyze our stories, mistakes, and shortcomings before losing any identification with them. Leaping before we have done our inner work correctly is useless and a considerable self-deception.

Being fully enlightened entails being fully human first. We incarnate to reach that stage through challenging and complex situations, emotions, and relationships in which we find ourselves entangled. Therefore, we must use them as the royal road to higher consciousness. Not because we have managed to keep away from them successfully, but because we have worked through them; we embody them to transcend them.

Life has the funny habit of repeatedly drawing people and situations into our lives to allow us to deal with the personal unconscious. Before getting to higher spiritual states, we must be aware of the darkness. Relationships can be compelling and challenging because we often project our unconscious wounds onto the other person. They frequently stem from childhood wounds that were never fully healed or past relationships from which we have not fully moved. It is because we have not been willing to see that we still carry burdens from the past. Occasionally, we are convinced that we have already worked through it and are healed, sane, and mature. At other times, we prefer to remain blind to our shortcomings since it is too painful to swim into the depths of our unconscious and admit our deficiencies. At times, it is just that too many triggers come at once, and we fall into mechanical reactions we thought were long overcome. More often than not, even if we are aware of these issues, we have never worked through them on a deep emotional level, and we cannot do it on our own. We require the guidance and assistance of a professional.

Therefore, we need to acknowledge that at some point, we have tried to avoid our psychological issues and do whatever it took to feel better about ourselves. Once we accept it, we can contemplate ourselves and others with greater compassion and understanding instead of criticizing and judging. We must recognize and act on addressing our darker or less spiritual emotions, impulses, and intentions and stop denying them as part of who we are. We must be aware of our need to be special, spiritual, and advanced, and stop dividing everything into positive and negative, higher and lower, spiritual and non-spiritual. We must stop wanting to reach a state of immunity to pain. Pain is inherent to the human condition. The sooner we acknowledge it, the earlier we can start working on not creating more suffering for ourselves and the world. We could stop looking for ways to suppress our problems without facing them head-on and stop ignoring the obvious fact that life is painful.

We should not overlook that the most widespread bypass in our society is the habit of remaining focused on practical reality at the expense of everything else. That illustrates an effort to avoid experiencing unity, the bigger picture, and the actual reality beyond conventional appearances. There is a shared obsession with achieving great success in the material world, often leading a spiritually bankrupt life. This would be a pragmatism bypass, one of the most dangerous illnesses of our times. And it is leading us into a hazardous situation, as we explained earlier in this book.

Chapter 11

Awakening

Jesus Christ knew he was God. So wake up and find out eventually who you really are. In our culture, of course, they'll say you're crazy and you're blasphemous, and they'll either put you in jail or in a nut house (which is pretty much the same thing). However, if you wake up in India and tell your friends and relations, "My goodness, I've just discovered that I'm God," they'll laugh and say, "Oh, congratulations, at last you found out."

Alan W. Watts

For many spiritual traditions, the journey to awakening is a gradual one. In Christianity, Judaism, and Islam, it is called salvation and is taught as a progressive path, except for their respective mystical branches. Some Eastern traditions have a more direct approach, such as Dzogchen and Mahamudra in Buddhism or Advaita Vedanta in Hinduism. It was not until the 1970s, when Eastern teachers came to the West, that those insights started to be included in the new schools of psychology and the teachings of some contemporary realized masters. The presence of realized individuals who came to their awakening through the direct approaches of what were once just Eastern paths is a recent phenomenon in Western culture. Fortunately, all this has allowed us to have access to ancient knowledge in a more modern manner. So people can understand it and start using it without having to move to India or the Himalayas to follow an authentic spiritual path. Realization is a real possibility for ordinary people living in a world of relationships, work, family, and everyday challenges.

The seemingly opposite notions of gradual and direct approaches can be misleading because those walking the direct path can take just as long to achieve stabilized realization as those on a gradual one. For example, many direct approaches require hours of arduous meditation and periods of retreat. The basis of the direct way is the emphasis on being present in the now, with total awareness as the starting point of transformation. At the same time, the gradual one emphasizes the need to cultivate virtues as the essential prerequisite.

What exactly is the meaning of awakening? We could say that it is the realization of one's true nature, in a way that the person's identity has shifted and stabilized, from the conditioned personality to that of his or her actual limitless being. The conditioned personality is the managerial ego full of habitual patterns and dualistic vision that we tend to believe is who we are, a separate entity with an independent existence. And the true nature is the essence of every individual, the divine spark: luminous, infinite, and complete. It is who we really are beyond the illusion of duality. It does not deny the body or the earthly life, yet there is a recognition that one's innermost identity is a fundamental awareness beyond all appearances and concepts.

Furthermore, it represents the core of our experience and our being and cannot be built because it preexists. Since conceptual thought processes are dualistic, it is not easy to translate a transcendental experience beyond any mental construction into words. It is helpful to understand that awakening is not an end in itself. It is the latest stage in human development, where the individual reaches their full potential. Indeed, it is the true purpose of our path and our life. Going beyond the apparent opposites of darkness and light, you can connect with a consciousness that can maintain unity amid both.

For the sake of understanding what it is like to dwell on the state of awakening, we will describe it. It is an experience in which there is no effort to be ourselves. Desires become transparent since there is no longer a need for anything. There is no action to maintain our identity; we are. There is no defense, judgment, or need to live up to any standard. It brings a dramatic decrease in psychological suffering. We perceive straightforwardly, without so many filters. We can act, feel, and think, but it is done from an authentic and spontaneous presence. Our tendency to both cling and reject dramatically drops.

We have no resistance to external events, no attachment to goals, no criticism of self or others, no grasping onto what we have, no fear about the future, and no struggle to become who we want to be because we are already that being. We feel uplifted, at peace, fulfilled, and whole. We finally discover what we have been looking for and arrive where we have always wanted to be. It is well beyond happiness. Being ourselves is a perfectly harmonious action equivalent to being One with all, beyond the boundaries of time and space. We can then see that the mind cannot understand the reality of the divine. It can only be felt. That is why these realizations are different from philosophical theories and ideas. They are direct and non-conceptual. The person becomes an embodiment of peace, stillness, and compassion. And this is a phenomenal feat. We can make an outstanding contribution to the unfolding era by remembering that every act of awakening consciousness benefits the whole.

Usually, it all starts with temporary experiences of oneness, where the person experiences reality without the mediation of analytical thought. They have direct contact with reality. As we described in the previous chapter, those ephemeral moments can already produce transformative effects on people. They no longer see any situation as a problem but as an opportunity. The experience of living in a state of harmony with life, enhanced awareness, a greater feeling of equanimity with sentient beings, and a resolve to serve are some of the things they can experience.

A convergence of the head center brings an increased capacity for understanding, knowingness, clarity, and intuitive guidance. Opening the heart center also creates the capacity for unconditional love, beingness, peace, vastness, vulnerability, and human connection. The opening of the solar plexus is often associated with an embodiment, inner power, groundedness, confidence, and trust. Through this movement, a progressive purification of the individual consciousness is frequently seen to occur, wherein false views are gradually abandoned, and new and more accurate perspectives of self and reality are formed. This process can take many years and helps to disintegrate the mental, emotional, and physical energy invested in defending our particular interpretation of who we are and what we need. Eventually, the feeling of being incomplete and the belief that something is missing in our life go away.

However, the integration and stabilization of those remarkable changes in everyday life is a challenging task. On the contrary, it represents a tremendous test for all of us. Psychologist John Selwood explains:

> Some of us who have been involved in meditative practices in the past few decades have a direct taste of realization... Seeing through the veils of the conditioned mind and realizing Being. The full embodiment of such realizations, a wise and balanced way of engaging in livelihood, intimate relationships, and the complex challenges of modern society, presents another hurdle altogether. We require other methods to help us integrate spiritual realization into our busy lives.

The goal of the spiritual path is not to have spiritual experiences but to use them to live a more spiritual life with more consciousness and change the world. Therefore, the main principle of integration is transforming one's personality into Being, which means carrying being into action.

Some teachers suggest that we make a distinction between awakening and realization. It can be a sudden or gradual awakening into a feeling of being part of a larger universe, from the belief that we are a separate, single entity into a clearer sense of being part of the infinite cosmos. On the other hand, realization occurs when that awakening has become a permanent state of being. Most people begin by describing moments or conditions of awakening, but then they dissolve and return to the identification with the personal. Liberation comes when we no longer connect to the little self and when there is no more searching. Since most people expect the awakening to be stable and lasting from the very beginning, I think it is essential to clarify this point since it can otherwise lead to suffering. It is just a common myth.

We must not have unrealistic expectations because most people struggle and search for inner rest for many years before the critical shift. And most people have to go through another long process before they can stabilize the realization of the unity of consciousness (if they can do it in the same lifetime).

There are quite a few misconceptions about what awakening is. Thus, it may be helpful to clarify them. It is not another spiritual experience or an induced and altered state of consciousness (sometimes by substances). We cannot accomplish it by sheer will, desire, or knowledge. Likewise, it is not a self-improvement undertaking. It is not a step toward becoming a better version of yourself because it transcends the ego. It is something radically different. It is a growing perception of inner silence and insight of no self or oneness. The person feels that the previous tendency to seek is over because of a shift of consciousness. The fact that they have found a home is confirmed.

It is also important to note that a person, sadly, does not immediately become extraordinary after awakening and cannot automatically transcend ordinary life experiences or all problematic emotions and circumstances. The issue is that there is no attachment anymore. Because everything is perceived as fleeting, flowing, and unfolding, things keep happening, but they no longer create suffering in the person. Grasping and fear are no longer superimposed on them. There is also a great surrendering to the whole, a letting go of all forms of control and letting life happen as it chooses to. All insecurities, fears, doubts, and a sense of personal deficiency are entirely dissolved.

For realization to be well-rooted, we must first go through and transform the structure of the ego, not just transcend it. That is, we have to face the narcissistic wound we all have, the profound hurt we carry for not having been seen, supported, and appreciated as we are. The wound of the heart that is born out of childhood conditioning will become a bigger spiritual problem if we do not take care of it. Working through this process can lead to feelings of betrayal by self and others, as well as feelings of void, rage or resentment, meaninglessness, and even existential depression. We can recognize it as part of the road if we know about it.

The false identification with our achievements, the pretense of being more developed than we are, and pride are some potential hindrances we must consider. Sometimes, we may be unwilling to enter the unknown because we are too attached to our beliefs and still identify with the stories we have created about ourselves. And an effort to maintain the state of realization may arise as if it were something that can be gained or lost by sheer force. We often fail to realize that emptiness does not lead to a nihilistic attitude but instead should be seen as what it really is — the universal soul, spirit, God, or source (in Western terms) or the clear light (in Buddhism) or Brahma (in Hinduism). In other words, complete peace and stillness without reflection, manifestation or projection; the essence of Being.

Those obstacles mentioned above can be overcome if we throw off ego ideals and come into alignment with and follow our inner guidance grounded in being—with transparency and humility.

How do you start the journey to awakening? Sometimes glimpses of it arise spontaneously. They can be recognized as mystical experiences, opening the doors of the spirit. Typically, you become aware of this possibility by being exposed to teachings on realization or meeting a teacher. Frequently, people have a persistent sense of hollowness that does not go away with any material achievement, perfect relationship, or distraction. Life seems meaningless, and people start wondering if there is something else. At times, we become like a child who outgrows the need to play with toys; the game is not interesting anymore. Keeping trapped in the madness of the material world and the instinctive pattern of trying to control or fix everything, everyone is perceived as useless. Many others go through really dark periods of failure or quiet desperation and feel they have come to the end of a line. If you still believe that you will find lasting happiness, satisfaction, or fulfillment in material objects, external activities, or relationships, the awakening will remain unreachable. Without realizing that nothing can complete you, you will not reach the spiritual maturity required.

In Eastern traditions, the role of a spiritual master on the path to enlightenment has always been highlighted and considered a must. It is recognized that when individuals think they do not need a teacher, it is because they are either arrogant or deluded or both. However, this does not match the Western mentality that values independence, autonomy, and an individual's will. Thus, this tends to be a delicate subject for us.

I have seen people in India—both Indians and Westerners— sit at the feet of a guru and expect a miracle to happen or boast about their connection with such an extraordinary being. Giving away one's power and responsibility to somebody else can be very comforting, so one gets rid of the burden of free will. This can often provide a false kind of security. Some of these gurus have attempted to cultivate an image of superhuman or avatar-like evolution to manipulate their followers, elevating themselves to a position of personal power. If awakening is not aligned with the purification and transformation of the ego, it becomes a super-ego. The borderline between self-realization and megalomania can be very thin.

In Buddhism, the dharma teacher or lama teaches others how to use different meditation techniques and explains Buddhist philosophy. An individual like this is not a guru since he does not usually put himself in a position of authority or power. Traditionally, a lama points out continuous instructions, provides support and guidance along the way, transmits knowledge and initiations, and helps anchor the truth he has already integrated.

The desire to discover our true self on our own is positive and necessary, the fuel of the self-development road. It is what will push us to start this road that is only sometimes straightforward. Every person on the path must eventually realize their fundamental limitations. Some areas of the trail cannot be accessed by any form of meditation or examination, for they cannot even be imagined. It is almost impossible to reach this transformation without a guide. Some people are in contact with living teachers and have a relationship with them. But in my experience, this is not always possible or necessary in our modern society, where such realized masters do not abound. At some point, guidance is needed, but it can be replaced by connecting with a teacher's books, videos, or audio.

Some people have moments of awakening, but without knowledge of spirituality or the different stages on the path, they may think they are crazy or forget what happened to them without looking into it further. To integrate and expand those experiences, we usually need someone who knows so that he or she can validate them for us. Otherwise, we may need to figure out what to do or what they mean.

We must take responsibility for our evolution, as progress depends on us. However, the path out of *samsara* is so tricky and twisted that without some profound guidance, we will stay trapped forever in our ignorance and illusions. The seeker needs to do the walking, but some sort of guide is beneficial when exploring the wild forest of the inner realm. It is advisable to have a map or a guide that warns us about the dangers and snares we may find, the valleys where we can rest, and the stairs that will take us to higher ground. Everybody's journey is in the same direction, and we have similar requirements to achieve inner peace and become whole. Our minor differences depend on our evolutionary past, karma, and potential; that is why we must choose the path and the pace more adapted to our idiosyncrasy. Ideally, we should have a being (personally present or through her works) with expertise, someone who has already gone through it and knows most of the subtleties.

Each person must be willing to make the necessary sacrifices to advance on the inner path, be ready to work hard, and leave aside whatever becomes a burden. Each person has a responsibility to follow the higher intention of his soul and commit to conquering his weaknesses. Each person needs a guide, and yet each one must walk alone. Each person needs to learn to use difficulties as the material for his growth and transformation. Of course, this is easier said than done. That is probably why many are called, but few are selected. This is not a path for those looking for a quick makeover or those not prepared to make a significant commitment.

Chapter 12

The role of meditation

When the meditation is mastered, the mind is unwavering like the flame of a candle in a windless place.

Bhagavad Gita

The role of meditation is vital in human transformation. Although Western culture prizes linear, discursive, and rational thought, meditation traditions from the East (Vedic, Tibetan Buddhism, China, and Japanese Buddhism, for instance) have procedures that lead to experiences beyond the conceptual mind. Those practices are meant to put the person in touch with the Absolute, beyond the division of subject and object, beyond duality. These are more direct modes of experience in which the knower and the known merge, bypassing the usual personal self-defense we hold on to. The goal is to remain in Cosmic consciousness, where you can still see the world and act in it, but your center of gravity is the presence. Through contemplative practice, one can enter increasingly into the great Silence.

The meditator learns only to notice the succession of thoughts, feelings, and sensations as they arise. In contrast to psychology and therapy, no attention is paid to the content. The person, therefore, is open to anything that appears in the mind without preference, comment, judgment, reflection, or interpretation. One of the first things we notice once we start meditating is that our mind (and therefore most of our day) is mainly dominated by verbal chatter. We start noticing that we spend all our time commenting on events and creating and repeating stories. It takes time and profound commitment to the practice to observe thoughts, images, ideas, fantasies, and theories as pictures of a movie projected on the screen of our head.

I genuinely agree with the view of the late Vietnamese master Thich Nhat Hanh:

> Meditation is to be aware of what is going on — in our bodies, in our feelings, in our minds, and in the world. Each day children die of hunger. Yet the sunrise is beautiful; the rose that bloomed this morning along the wall is a miracle. Life is both dreadful and wonderful. To practice meditation is to be in touch with both aspects.

Meditation is a tool that can help us achieve a psychological and emotional balance, preparing us to face life's challenges without being swept away by them. Our day is filled with so much information that we need structure and discipline to keep us sane.

As mentioned, meditation teaches us to let go of the fixations of surface thoughts and sensations by allowing them to arise without following or reacting to them. Instead of finding meaning and solutions to whatever shows up in our minds, we release the little world of continuous self-preoccupation and embrace the larger world around us. It is a preparation to maintain a radical opening to whatever experience comes to you, too, instead of stepping back, hiding from it, or even engaging in inner inquiry all the time. Working on this new approach can direct us toward developing a real presence. When you learn to have a direct and honest relationship with what it is without trying to make it different, a new kind of awareness, joy, and clarity is born in you. It is like discovering unknown freedom that has always been available yet concealed from you. It gives you inner strength and trust in life and yourself. Not only that, but it fills you with deep serenity. You discover that everything you ever wanted is already in you.

There are over 3,000 scientific studies on the benefits of meditation. Some of those verified benefits include decreasing depression, less ruminative thinking and dysfunctional beliefs; it can be as effective to treat anxiety as antidepressant drug therapy without any side effects, reduces stress and anxiety in general, increases activity in areas of the brain involved in learning and memory, regulates emotions, sense of self, and gives perspective, improves focus, attention, and ability to work under stress, provides better processing of information, making decisions, forming memories and improving concentration; increases mental strength, resilience, and emotional intelligence; relieves pain better than morphine, reduces hyperactivity and impulsivity, improves your mood and psychological wellbeing, prepares you to deal with stressful events, fosters creativity, reduces the risk of heart disease and stroke, develops a higher immunity in the system and resilience to stress, decreases inflammatory disorders, reduces blood pressure, and it may even make you live longer. If, after this long list, you are not convinced of the importance of practicing meditation, you are a lost cause. It is fantastic that we have solid scientific research that shows what Eastern philosophies have known for centuries: meditation should be a part of our daily lives because it helps us in many ways, some of which are obvious and some less obvious.

The less tangible or evident effects are even more critical because they form the base of our path toward enlightenment. And they have to do with transcending the body and mind to experience more profound aspects of our self. We are dominated by everything with which our ego becomes identified. Until we can achieve a certain degree of psychological detachment from our thoughts, we cannot transcend them and explore more profound realms of being. As long as we are dragged by the compulsions and defenses of the ego, we cannot step out of it at will. Higher awareness remains hidden from us as long as we identify with the ups and downs of our thoughts and emotions. If we consider ourselves to be our accomplishments and failures, we are still slaves to society's rules, which try to control us. As long as we feed our constructed stories about who we are, the possibility of transcendence remains elusive.

We require training in meditation to surpass the theoretical and analytical mind. Entering into the realm of experience is the necessary bridge to integrate life lessons and rise beyond the sensory world, not being lured by appearances and sensory perceptions. In meditation, we can feel what it is like to have direct contact with a larger and deeper reality without the continuous interpretation of the mind. Direct contact with the energy that surrounds all, without any self-seeking or self-enhancement activities, with the underlying peace and perfection in and around us. It enables one to go beyond words and traditional concepts into pure consciousness. We can experience a state of embracing and fullness without having to do anything. It can actually help us to have deep insights and stay in a state of no ego. It is a beautiful key to learning to surrender. Of course, formal meditation is only a stepping stone to preparing the ground so we can live all that during our daily lives. This would be the goal of meditation.

We are introducing it in the West with baby steps. In such a skeptical, materialistic, and utilitarian society, it is mainly presented as mindfulness, a simple method of mind training. When transplanted to our Western culture, this type of meditation has been lifted out of its larger context of a culture permeated by Buddhist values and ethics. It is also a part of the training system and, even more, a way of life. When this form of meditation is practiced as a mind exercise, isolated from other aspects of the Buddhist path, factors such as the right intention, the cultivation of ethical behavior, and the proper understanding are often disregarded. In my opinion, this can have negative consequences. That is why we should not speak of and encourage "mindfulness" but "caring mindfulness." Otherwise, we may end up with mindful shooters and mindful psychopaths.

Meditation has to be practiced daily. It is not so much about the length of time spent meditating. It is more about having the discipline to do it every day. Otherwise, the possibility of transformation is unreachable, lost in a hurry, and a mindless repetition of daily activity. It is also an excellent way to connect with our deeper selves and counteract the damaging effects of excessive thinking. Staying hooked on continuous judging and analyzing and feeding on more useless information takes us nowhere.

I hope that most people who begin practicing, even simply for the urgent need to alleviate their stress and suffering, will eventually want to deepen their practice and assimilate it as a spiritual path. Voltaire already knew: "Meditation is the dissolution of thoughts in Eternal awareness or Pure consciousness without objectification, knowing without thinking, merging finitude in infinity."

Chapter 13

Leaving the Matrix

Know all things to be like this:

A mirage, a cloud castle, a dream, an apparition, without essence, but with qualities that can be seen...

As a magician makes illusions of horses, oxen, carts, and other things, nothing is as it appears.

Buddha

The movie *The Matrix* provided an excellent framework for understanding that we are born into an illusory, dreamlike world and can take a red pill to wake up from this simulated reality. It shows that our three-dimensional world is not what we think it is. If the cognitive dissonance mechanism does not take over your mind, you start appreciating alternative models from the ones presented to you by society. Once you perceive the world differently, you understand that the so-called reality is a commonly held system. Ralph Waldo Emerson once noted that the mind could not return to its former state once it expanded to new dimensions. So, once you see the glitches of the Matrix, you begin the path toward departure.

It has been found that the brain responds to perceived stimuli in a virtual environment the same way it does to natural impulses in a physical environment. Today, technology is so advanced that fully immersive virtual-world simulations can be compelling. A tempting metaverse is ready to unfold for those eager to step into an artificial timeline.

The world around us is a physical construct, as some scientists have presented. The physical world does not consist of physical matter but of information.

Some cutting-edge scientists and theorists have formulated the Simulation Hypothesis, which states that we all live inside a sophisticated video game. In this simulation—they say—there are player characters inside the rendered world who are associated with and controlled by conscious beings (biological or otherwise) outside the generated world. Inside, there are also non-player characters who are there to do what usual non-player characters do in video games: assist the players in some way to achieve, or hinder, their goals.

While we have to look hard for ways that the simulation hypothesis might be connected to some core beliefs of Western religions, the simulation hypothesis is much clearer in Eastern traditions.

Buddha did not say much about God. He did not affirm that there was or was not a God or gods. He was just silent on the subject. Instead, he seemed more concerned with the mechanics of how life, reincarnation, and karma worked and what this meant for the person. Eastern traditions teach that the world around us is a sort of illusion, like a dream. We use our bodies to play different roles in our multiple lives. It is very similar to a very sophisticated video game, like the *Matrix* movie.

The Eastern traditions explicitly support the notion that the world around us is *maya* or an illusion and that our actions are recorded and have reverberations that must be played out, often in future lives.

According to the Hindu Vedas, Lila is the grand play. We become so involved in it that we take it for reality. Of course, a stage play is a metaphor that made sense when it was written. A more modern allegory for us is that of a video game. This play is not just a movie we watch comfortably seated among the public. On the contrary, we actively participate, modifying it.

In Buddhism, the whole point is to recognize the illusory nature of the world around us, *samsara*, as if we were in a dream.

There is an entire practice, Dream Yoga, within the Tibetan traditions whose goal is to help you recognize that you are in a dream while you are asleep. Once you realize that all dream states are merely illusory, you will be prepared to do the same while awake. It is one of the Six Yogas of Naropa, preserved in Tibetan traditions.

Humans have never fully explored the more profound meaning of this metaphor, which has been used for hundreds of thousands of years. We have yet to fully integrate the idea that what we perceive to be real is a kind of projection, like an interactive artificial movie experience reminiscent of a dream. Or even more accurately, we could say it is just like a video game or a well-developed simulation.

In Buddhism, the idea is to reach enlightenment, to get off the wheel of reincarnation, by waking up from *samsara*. Let's remember that "Buddha" literally means "one who is awake."

Since the beginning, video games have used the idea of having multiple lives to keep playing, which is a clear metaphor for reincarnation. As Eastern traditions explain, a soul downloads to a physical body repetitively. They use the colorful analogy of crossing the River of Forgetfulness, so we cannot remember our past lives. We then incarnate in a new body, and in so doing, we go through new experiences, creating new karma as we go through new situations in the game. The Buddhist philosophy is expressed in Buddha's endless wheel of wandering, or *samsara*, where people get caught for a very long time.

In video games, people are players who live outside the rendered world. They play a character in the game world, and they can pause the character or keep playing it until it dies. By taking action in this life, we are creating a new set of quests for our soul to complete in the future life. That is the law of karma in action. Therefore, each time we play the game, we generate more challenges to fulfill. An interaction is initiated when the players' souls feel ready to accept the challenges. Free will and choice are present, and so is the invisible force that guides us toward certain people and specific actions to allow us to balance our karma. When the person awakens to the reality of the illusory state, Buddhists explain that the wheel of wandering stops turning. The individual consciousness has completed the cycle; the drop is then free to return to the ocean. Thus, they are in their last incarnation here in the game.

Making things a bit more complicated, my insights have led me to see that far from living in a single universe, we live in a complex, interconnected network of multiple timelines. This concept is currently known as the multiverse. The multiverse warps our understanding of the world around us and our knowledge of the past and the future. Consequently, neither space nor time is what we believe it is.

Not just one timeline can be simulated, but several—or even an infinite number. Each simulated timeline will be a different simulation run, with some variables changing based on new rules, according to the levels of consciousness of the souls participating.

This may seem far-fetched, if not a logical impossibility, from our typical everyday experience. Nonetheless, from the perspective of a simulated world, the idea of multiple timelines extending from multiple pasts into multiple futures and dimensions is plausible. The multiverse idea is quite common now in the world of physics. It is called the parallel universe theory or the quantum multiverse. It explains the phenomenon of quantum indeterminacy. This interpretation of quantum mechanics suggests that every time a quantum measurement is made, the universe splits into an almost infinite number of parallel universes, each with a different shared history. This proposes a map of the other possible states of the universe and the possible interconnecting timelines.

Science fiction and visionary author Philip K. Dick wrote: "We are living in a computer-programmed reality, and the only clue we have to it is when some variable is changed, and some alteration in our reality occurs." When you can perceive — usually through deep questioning and long-term meditation — that the everyday world is an illusion, you see with astonishing clarity that there cannot be one objective reality. At that point, you conclude that everything is a matter of perception. Then the commonly accepted paradigm shatters into a million pieces, the ground under your feet disappears, and you are on your own.

We come to this demanding simulation called Earth not to repress our human traits. We come here to fully experience what it means to live in such a low-vibrational dualistic world and emerge from it enriched and polished. Our goal is not to stay alive but to keep being human. Only when we can see through the falsehood of separation and the obsession for survival, and when we embody the sort of compassion that recognizes the oneness of all life, will we be able to transcend this dimension forever. Once the lessons are learned, you do not require repeating the intensive course. Once you graduate, you are ready for more advanced games.

The rational mind is not the one in charge of this process. This can only be achieved through direct or mystical experiences, often brought about through the heart and inner self-realization. You see, and you know, whether others publicly recognize this or not.

Things are very different from what they appear to be. Our perception is biased by what we have been taught to be true. Today, the great majority of people generally accept myths told by convincing scientists or prominent experts without hesitation. We go through the motions like sleepwalkers, conforming to any rule, bending down to false kings and popes, and idolizing celebrities who have sold their souls to the devil. Hence, we reinforce the shared dream and get increasingly trapped in it.

Until your level of consciousness allows you to have glimpses of Reality. Once you have strengthened your connection with the Universal Mind, the previously solid pillars that sustain the simulation start to thin out. Synchronicities and further insights begin to pile up, confirming intuitions and hunches. You start distinguishing the voice of your inner guidance during your greater silence. Answers begin to show up because you dare to ask questions. Unbeknown to most, physical reality loses its grip on you.

Dramas and rollercoaster reactions are replaced by a neutral attitude that faces each situation with equanimity. Unbridled passions and compulsions get tamed. Inner vision becomes the primary compass. More and more pieces of the universal puzzle make sense. You see this world as a theater where global and personal backgrounds and circumstances are provided for your own realization. You can understand that you are the main character of your play. Instead of becoming entangled in the minutiae of the story, you become aware that it is just a well-designed construction intended to fool you into becoming immersed in the play. Therefore, you laugh at your myopia, forgive the other players who were fulfilling their roles to help you develop, and become the actor without stopping the play. Then, the Infinite Plan shines through the cracks of human suffering and foolishness. Eventually, everyone will realize that we chose this situation ourselves and will have the means to cut through the prison walls. Our Spirit felt that the current avatar would greatly benefit from this intense course on duality. Therefore, the expedition began.

We all need to take this solo journey to reconnect with the ground of eternal Being.

Chapter 14

Wise people

A hero is born among a hundred, a wise man is found among a thousand, but an accomplished one might not be found even among a hundred thousand men.

Plato

Wisdom is the quality that distinguishes great leaders from the rest, who may be good professionals or even famous people. According to research, the correlation between age and wisdom is nil between the ages of 25 and 75. Why? Because wisdom emerges not from experience but from reflecting deeply on the lessons gained from experience. As we have seen before, wisdom is only present when we let go of our ego obsessions and ambitions. As psychologist Robert Sternberg explained: "Wisdom and egocentricity are incompatible... People who [are wise] have gotten where they are by taking other people's interests into account." These remarkable beings have a loving way of being in the world. It is impossible to truly judge from the outside since external behavior is less important than inner motivation and the sincerity of their intent. What the person feels inside is far more crucial than what is shown outside.

Of course, wisdom also requires being able to challenge the status quo when necessary and renounce external approval (and in some cases risk total rejection) to fulfill a purpose in alignment with essential values that makes the best use of this human life.

The new leaders of the current society need to be wise. They must move people emotionally through inspiration, making them feel touched or significantly changed. But also physically:

encouraging people to act differently, and mentally, generating new insights and strategies about how to live in our world.

The good news is that we already have some accomplished individuals with these characteristics. They are at the forefront, leading by example, without wishing to have followers or build personal marketing. However, the rest of humanity does require more role models and visionaries like them to show the direction toward the highest stages. It is important to have examples from our culture and time because although plenty of people throughout history have led exemplary lives and left a crucial legacy, individuals now need to be able to relate to the wisest. They must feel that the wise are like them, living in a contemporary and complex world, in order to believe that achieving their high level of development is not only possible but also feasible. Otherwise, most people will consider them too different from their present-day selves and, therefore, not valid representations of who they are at this age.

Therefore, the individuals selected to be discussed here are only a few models relevant to people in the West. Many other anonymous people are currently enriching humanity, dealing with immediate difficulties without losing sight of long-term goals. They are highly aware individuals who can speak to both the minds and the hearts of people. I want to show that we all can become wise if they have done it. We all have the seed of greatness.

Simon Parkes

I discovered Simon Parkes during the Covid circus. He was one of the few people who truly knew what he was talking about and was generous enough to expose himself, sharing his truth, privileged information, and a spiritual perspective on everything going on at the time. His calm demeanor and steadfast confidence inspired many people who were losing faith in the face of a great deal of darkness and fear on our planet.

Founder of the humanitarian and spiritual grassroots organization Connecting Consciousness, he embodies the characteristics and values of what I see as leaders on the new earth.

He was brought up in a very unusual environment; his grandfather had worked in the British Secret Intelligence Service (MI6), and his mother for the MI5 branch of the same security service. Having to be extremely careful with the people she related to, she did not have friends, boyfriends, or remarry, but she provided Simon with a solid set of values and principles to base his life upon. She insisted that Simon be exposed to good role models and positive outcomes, even when watching television. Therefore, he was taught very early on how critical it is to be loyal and sovereign and always to do the right thing, despite personal consequences.

This proved a valuable and distinctive hallmark in his career as a politician in the 1980s and 1990s. When he served two terms as an elected politician in London and then in a rural area, he faced numerous difficulties trying to improve the citizens' lives. He discovered firsthand that it is tough to remain honest and incorruptible if you get seriously involved in politics nowadays. Thus, he preferred to leave that aside and try to help others in a more spiritual manner.

As he always had an exceptional connection with higher realms, he could see life from a bigger-picture perspective. Being so connected to the different dimensions where our consciousness exists could have led him to choose a monastic way of life, bathing in the bliss of such a blessing. However, instead of becoming a solitary guru without the need to interact with others, he took the most challenging path, helping others by modeling what it is like to be highly evolved yet involved in Western society. That is probably the most effective instruction one can give, to teach by example.

Unlike most people's psychic abilities while on a spiritual quest, his did not show up due to his spiritual development. He was born with those talents because of his efforts in previous lifetimes. Therefore, his inner search had to do more with finding a way to impact the world around him, positively, with his gifts and yet not become a prisoner of this dual world. In other words, how to maintain his independence without hating the world as it is right now. I think that many people who read this book can relate to this conundrum: How can you avoid being used by the system, but shape the world around you, and not become full of anger against the injustices, indoctrination, and abuse of power?

After leaving high-level politics, he became more involved in sharing spiritual development teachings. In 2015, he was approached by very influential people who had broadly told him what was coming in the future of humanity, which is actually happening now. He then decided to build a strong framework that could take the problems we are facing nowadays. That is how the Connecting Consciousness organization was born: to go beyond people's material needs and provide a community of aware individuals who believe in the truth, in being sovereign under any circumstance, and who can support each other on the complex path of being awake in this chaotic world. This voluntary organization has thousands of members worldwide in over 100 countries. It is refreshing to find a place where thinking out of the box is not belittled, where there are others aware that the system around us is not designed to support us but is created to control us, and where people genuinely believe that there is a different way of doing things and are committed to implementing that.

Leading such an organization on his own, with the help of his wife, entails such a level of dedication that he no longer has what we call a normal life. He does not enjoy the freedom and time to do much anymore. Still, he takes it with great equanimity, since he believes that this is his calling, what his soul prepared him for, and what he has signed up for in this lifetime: to prioritize his service to others, regardless of the repercussions on his personal life and comfort.

During the exciting conversation I had with Simon to prepare for this brief biography, it became clear that he is a Bodhisattva, one of those spiritually heroic persons who personify the virtues of wisdom and compassion. A beacon of light devoted to benefiting others, opening doors so that people can cross the threshold, connecting and supporting the daring but lonely ones who do not wish to get swallowed up by the "Matrix," presenting and manifesting a vision of a new earth, where human beings live for the benefit of all.

Bill Thetford

Bill was a professor of medical psychology at Columbia University in New York, eminent in his field and known for his research into personality theory. He was also a partner in the original transcription of *A Course in Miracles* (ACIM) and a true practitioner of its teachings. His practice of forgiveness, his kind presence, and his great sense of humor all led to his ultimate realization. Thanks to the beautiful biography Carol Howe wrote, we can get more insight into his path. Although he died in 1988, his life was so contemporary that we can consider him an example of what we can achieve in this life, regardless of our circumstances and responsibilities.

As a child, he lost his sisters and contracted severe scarlet fever, which led to rheumatic fever and a debilitating heart condition, so he had to stay in bed for a very long time. It allowed him to learn the art of acceptance at an early age. He started pondering profound questions such as "Who am I?" and "What is life's purpose?"

Bill received a Ph.D. in psychology and was recruited by the CIA. Because his training involved working with leading-edge scientists and innovators in science and medicine, he became widely recognized and respected throughout his field. Thus, he was hired in 1951 as one of ten senior psychologists. His duties entailed administering various tests to applicants seeking to become intelligence officers and spies and then interviewing and recommending them. He only stayed for a couple of years and then moved on. He ended up at Columbia University as head of the psychological research program and as assistant professor of psychology in the Department of Psychiatry. The circumstances there at the time were complicated. His colleagues were suspicious and hostile, the atmosphere was chaotic, and the task was overwhelming. Bill probably contributed to the problems by projecting his judgments, fears, unconscious conditioning, and unexamined assumptions like we all do.

As *A Course in Miracles* says, "Tolerance for pain may be high, but it is not without limit. Eventually, everyone begins to recognize, however dimly, that there must be a better way." He was suffering so much that something had to give. He said, "There must be a better way, and I'm determined to find it." This took a significant amount of effort initially, but he did succeed eventually. Tensions lessened, and enmity dropped away. It was the beginning of essential developments in his life. Helen Schucman, his closest colleague and friend, started transcribing *A Course in Miracles*, following the dictation of a voice she was internally hearing and identified as Jesus. For seven years, he directly assisted her in finishing and editing the work and later publishing it. Although Bill had not been interested in religious or spiritual matters before ACIM dictation began, he recognized the material's universal nature. Consequently, he began an earnest inquiry into the world's major religious traditions and teachings.

His particular role in bringing that outstanding book into the world did not give him a free pass to enlightenment. His life was quite a mess despite his intellectual brilliance and professional accomplishments. He understood that he had to apply what appeared in the book to progress. Bill was determined to heal his attitudes and practice working on the dissolution of his ego, changing his mind from fear and guilt to love and from holding resentments to kindness. Like all of us, he began with a partial dedication. Still, instead of resting on his academic laurels, thinking that his job was done once the book was published, he decided to move away from his role as a respected professor and make his primary goal the practice of forgiveness.

He gave up his research on the ego, which he considered his most significant academic contribution. He also realized that he could not stay at Columbia University once the book went public since it was potentially an awkward situation in his professional environment. However, Bill never desired to be in the spotlight, and he permanently withdrew from public attention, even when ACIM became well known. He avoided everything that would bring him notoriety related to it.

Of course, he had to confront his fears about leaving the prestige associated with Columbia, his tenure and hard-to-attain position, and financial security. He decided to move to California and abandoned his life, career, and the person he had been until then. That time was over. He even gave up all ties with friends and acquaintances of many years, both professional and social, as if clearing the decks for the final challenge of his life: to fully concentrate on the practice of forgiveness and letting go of the ego. Even if no one else understood Bill's intention, he followed his inner guidance, devoting himself as best he could to his healing, trying to untangle and remove all accumulated mental debris. For years, he was still harboring some grievances, although his kind nature was always present, his light shining through, and his help unfailingly available. It is reassuring to know we do not have to wait until we are entirely healed and realized before we decide to be of real help. The point is to be compassionate, open, and nonjudgmental, recognizing that our job is not correcting others but loving them as they are.

Bill operated from a deep sense of integrity, which probably accounts for the immediate sense of safety almost everyone felt around him. He put no weight on degrees or fame or anything of the sort. He did not need to defend, impress, convince, or dominate. Although highly complex, he never flaunted his intellectual brilliance, yet he had a profound and universal understanding of human beings and how we grow and develop. Although he had not resolved all his psychological and spiritual difficulties, he worked as hard as possible to have an entire spiritual life. He truly desired to give up the ego-enhancing and defensive needs to be correct, to feel protected, or to prove his value, trying very hard not to take things personally, and recognizing what did and did not matter. As his focus on the intellect as a source of power and wisdom diminished, his mind grew quieter. In a world where so few people are dedicated to releasing their grievances and living without resistance, he is an excellent example of what we can achieve when prioritizing our inner development.

Bill modeled how we can be helpful to each other without being oppressive, without giving unrequited advice, or trying to fix people. He touched others deeply because his objective was to be aware of their underlying love, and he was determined to let go of judgment. He never tried to impose his views on anybody. As he was very accepting, people felt relaxed, safe, and loved in his presence.

At the end of his life, he had finally taken down the psychological boundaries by which he had defined himself for so long. By doing so, he had forgiven himself for all past mistakes. He went from being controlled, reserved, and rigid to becoming expansive, flowing, and flexible. He willingly stripped himself of his psychological armor, esteem, damaging habits, and prejudices. He became a humble and enlightened teacher by his being and by his grace, kindness, and love. When he died of a massive heart attack, he was finally free. Bill understood that the most remarkable thing we can do to help the world is to awaken ourselves.

Jetsunma Tenzin Palmo

She became famous worldwide through the book *A Cave in the Snow*, narrating her quest to attain realization in a female body. She set an unprecedented example of following in the footsteps of the most dedicated Tibetan yogis by spending 12 years in a solitary retreat in a cave in Ladakh, in the Indian Himalayas.

She was born in London. Even as a child, she was interested in spiritual matters and unusually fascinated by Asia. She studied Christianity, Judaism, and Hinduism. Later, she had a good job as a librarian. When she was 18, she and her mother were delayed at an airport for eight hours. The only book she had with her from the library was one about Buddhism. Right there, she realized she was a Buddhist. At 20, she embarked on a cargo ship for a two-week journey that took her to Bombay; she then went on to northern India, where she found a position as an English teacher in a school for young lamas. She worked there for a few months before meeting her master. She became the second Western woman ordained in the Tibetan Buddhist tradition three weeks after meeting him. She lived at a monastery for six years as the only nun among 100 monks. She could see the discrimination that restricted women's access to teachings that were imparted freely to men.

In 1976, she started living in a small cave in the Himalayas and remained there for 12 years, even if local people tried to dissuade her, advising that it was not safe for her to be alone. The cave she chose was situated at an altitude of 4,300 meters, difficult to access. She grew her food during the retreat and carried on uninterrupted intense spiritual practice and deep meditation. Following Buddhist directions for this kind of solitary retreat, she never lay down, sleeping in a traditional wooden meditation box in a meditative upright posture. From time to time, she went down to the monastery to listen to teachings, get food supplies, and talk to her lama. She spent the summers preparing for the long winters when she was utterly cut off. But after nine years, she decided to spend the three following years in complete isolation. She survived temperatures below 35°C and continuous snow for six to eight months of the year. Once, a big blizzard raged for seven days and nights, the snow covered the cave door, and she thought she would die. She was not at all afraid. She says the retreat helped her develop inner resourcefulness and confidence, learning to cope with whatever happened.

Afterward, she moved to Italy for a while and eventually decided to teach to raise funds to build a nunnery in India. In this place, women could study and train because women have been spiritually overlooked for too long. In 2000, she founded that nunnery, finally allowing young nuns to realize their intellectual and spiritual potential. In 2008, Tenzin Palmo got the title of Jetsunma (reverend lady) to recognize her spiritual growth and work in promoting female practitioners' status in Tibetan Buddhism.

During my first stay in Dharamshala (India) many years ago, I was fortunate enough to attend a couple of lectures given by her. I was so inspired by her courage, depth, and wisdom. She has a presence that touches your heart beyond the words she utters. I remember her last sentence that embodies her beautifully: "From now on, there is nothing you cannot accomplish in a woman's body." Very promising in a world with still so much discrimination and subjugation of women.

Eckhart Tolle

He was born in Germany. At age 13, he moved to Spain to live with his father. He had no formal education between 13 and 22 since he refused to attend school. He felt it was a hostile environment and would rather not be part of it. His father was unconventional, allowing him to pursue his particular interests, such as literature and languages. Only at 22 did he become interested in intellectual matters like philosophy and psychology. He admits to not having had a happy childhood since his parents were in constant conflict. He was more comfortable in Spain, working as a tourist guide and a language teacher for a few years. However, at the age of 29, he went through recurrent periods of depression and anxiety. He studied at the University of London and went to Cambridge to do research as a postgraduate student with a scholarship. But he admits that the motivation behind his academic achievement was fear and unhappiness.

Shortly after his twenty-ninth birthday, one night, he felt so much despair that it was almost unbearable. He thought he could no longer live with himself. At that point, he started to question who was that self that he would not live with and who he really was, one or two. He noticed there were two. There was a miserable "I" that he wholly identified with, and something else more profound. He could see the eternal "Beingness" or pure consciousness before identification with form. At that moment, there was a last glimpse of intense fear as he was losing the self, feeling sucked into an internal void. He decided not to resist, and then fear disappeared. The following day, he woke up in a state of total inner peace and bliss, something he had never experienced in his entire life. Afterward, he says that his thoughts were reduced by about 80–90%, so he spent much time walking around in a state of inner stillness.

Consequently, he started to lose interest in his research. He abandoned academia, drifting for two years, staying with friends or occasionally in a Buddhist monastery, and sitting on park benches most of his time. It took him ten years to fully understand what this transformation meant and translate it into spiritual teachings.

Although the publication of his first book, *The Power of Now*, in 1999 started very modestly, after being recommended by Oprah Winfrey on her TV show it became a *New York Times* bestseller and an international success for years, translated into 33 languages. Later on, a ten-week online seminar Oprah hosted with him, commenting on one chapter of his book, *A New Earth*, each week, was viewed by 11 million people daily. Something difficult to imagine with such a spiritual book and message. Despite his enormous success and recognition, he remains humble, without any trace of pretense, and with no plans to build a commercial empire out of his teachings.

His philosophy explains with great simplicity how to overcome the feeling of separation, the meaning of surrender, and how to avoid suffering and detach from your thoughts by living in the now. In his own words:

Happiness is achieved when you are One with life. Being one with life is being one with now. You then realize that you don't live your life, but life lives you. Life is the dancer, and you are the dance.

He has the remarkable gift of making people realize that we can keep in touch with the deepest source of our being out of the ordinary events of the day. He affirms that Descartes's central insight—I think, therefore I am—one of the foundations of Western thinking, is fundamentally wrong. Being immersed in such a rational left-brain society, it is very challenging to question that thinking is not the core of who we are and that we are the formless presence beyond time instead.

When I attended an intense retreat and teachings with Eckhart in a bucolic place in the woods of upstate New York, I could confirm that regardless of his shyness and lack of exuberant charisma, he has a presence of peace that fills the place he enters. You can tell he is one of those wise individuals that have the virtue to impact millions of people positively. He is a modern mystic, continuously rooted in the present, in a state of connectedness and inner stillness.

Matthieu Ricard

He was born in France. His father was a renowned French philosopher, and his mother, a painter, grew up in Parisian intellectual circles. After watching documentaries on great spiritual teachers in India when he was 20, he traveled there. The encounters with them left an indelible impression on him. He kept going back and forth for a few years, but following his master's advice, he did not quit his studies immediately. After earning a doctorate in molecular biology from the prestigious Pasteur Institute in Paris, Ricard left and moved to Darjeeling to study with his Tibetan teacher and became a monk. He likes to mention that he met quite extraordinary people in his youth (like Igor Stravinsky and Luis Buñuel), all well known for their achievements but not showing similar excellence on the human side. It was not until he met Tibetan lamas that he found a trustworthy source of inspiration and exemplary human beings.

Matthieu is an author and photographer too. The dialogue with his father (Jean-François Revel), *The Monk and the Philosopher*, was a bestseller in Europe and was translated into 21 languages.

He tirelessly warns about not blindly sacrificing the world we hand down to our children in favor of our short-term selfish wants and desires. Everywhere he goes, he insists on promoting altruism through education, institutions that respect every individual's rights, and political and economic systems that allow everyone to flourish without sacrificing the good of future generations.

He owns very little. He lives six months out of the year in Nepal, partly at his monastery near Kathmandu, and doing a two- or three-month retreat each winter in a tiny hermitage without any heating. He spends much time traveling around the globe, advocating for cooperation, altruism, and the need to transform ourselves to serve others better. He also runs a small humanitarian nongovernmental organization (NGO), to which all the revenue from his book sales and speaker fees is donated. In addition, he actively contributes to the research on the effect of meditation on the brain at various universities in the USA and Europe. He co-authors scientific publications on these topics.

After participating in a 12-year brain study on meditation and compassion led by the University of Wisconsin, researchers found that his brain waves and activity were off the happiness charts. The media labeled him "the happiest man in the world." After the sudden fame, he felt torn between living a life of seclusion or as a Buddhist media star. One day, he asked the Dalai Lama (for whom he translates into French at his public appearances in French-speaking countries) if he could go on an extended retreat, longing to disappear from the public eye. But he was assured that it was not time yet: "The world is in pain, and what you can do and is most necessary to do right now is to try to communicate a cure."

In a way, he has become a great interpreter of Buddhism for people in the West, but without compromising the core of the philosophy, being straightforward about the roots of our misery:

> Once we deconstruct our egos, we could truly begin to see the world as a place inhabited by other people, some who might need our help. This dissolving becomes then all-powerful... Our attachment to the ego is fundamentally linked to the suffering we feel and the suffering we inflict on others. Freedom is the opposite.

I met Matthieu many years ago when I took six months off and lived in Nepal to concentrate on writing my first published book, *Cuando Sea Feliz*, and to carry out some meditation retreats. I stayed most of my time at a guest house in his Shechen monastery, and I will never forget the mix of benevolence and firmness he exuded. He is a model of wisdom and an embodiment of true happiness.

Byron Katie

She was born in Texas and raised in a small desert town in California in the years following World War II. She became a competitive teenager who sought to be the best in everything she did. She married at 19 and had three kids soon afterward. She blamed herself when her marriage had difficulties, being a perfectionist and a high achiever. Thus, she focused on becoming materially successful in compensation. She and her husband invested in real estate, and in the 1970s Katie became a millionaire. However, she felt it was not enough, as it was not satisfying. Her obsession with being happy through money and power only increased her frustration and rage. This started to put a strain on the relationship with her children and husband, and the marriage ended in divorce. Then she married again, and being in a new loving relationship made her feel better for a while. But it did not last. Her life had no meaning. She tried to soothe her darkness and misery with food, alcohol, tobacco, and constant striving, to no avail. She went weeks without bathing, changing her clothes, or brushing her teeth. For almost ten years, she was in chronic depression, without being able even to leave her room for two years, and considered suicide to be her only way to break free from desperation. She used to sleep with a gun under her pillow. She became so agoraphobic and paranoid that her husband sent her to a halfway house. There, the other women were so afraid of her that she was placed in an attic. She had such low self-esteem and so much self-hatred that she slept on the floor because she did not believe she deserved a bed.

At 43, she experienced an astonishing moment of clarity that transformed her life as she lay sleeping on the floor and a cockroach crawled over her foot. At that moment, she realized that no thought was true, so the world the self interpreted was unreal. It was all imagined. She underwent a total shift in her mind, no longer identifying with her former self. She was a different person.

She had to keep her realization quiet for seven years to sustain it, as she could not put it into words. She just felt overwhelmed by unconditional love. Eventually, thoughts returned, and so did judgments, fears, and expectations. When that occurred, she could see herself slipping from the freedom of her awakening into the mind of suffering. But she learned to start questioning her thoughts, which is how her world changed, making her appreciate the universe as kind and generous, noticing that what keeps the mind busy is trying to prove the universe is hostile. She found freedom by agreeing with life, without offering any resistance, "wanting what you have and loving what it is," as the key to ending separation.

She developed "The Work," a simple method of self-inquiry and learning to become responsible for our happiness and allowing others to be responsible for their own. She thinks we must question our thoughts to break the spell and wake ourselves up. She demonstrates at her workshops and in her books that:

> If your beliefs are stressful, and you question them, you come to see that they aren't true—whereas before questioning, you absolutely believe them. How can you live in joy when believing thoughts that bring sadness, frustration, anger, alienation, and loneliness? When you believe those thoughts, you think that the world is making you unhappy. But it's your thoughts about the world that are making you unhappy.

Now, she lives in a state of grace, maintaining that our world is 100% our responsibility. She is a woman who shines joy, continually surrendering to life as it arises in the present moment.

Chapter 15

Where to start

Spiritual opening is not a withdrawal to some imagined realm or safe cave. It is not a pulling away, but a touching of all the experience of life with wisdom and with a heart of kindness, without separation.

Jack Kornfield

We incarnate on Earth, having to play the game of existence with unknown rules. We gradually start building a mental map and worldview to help us travel and understand our society and culture. Wise people also have to go through this. The difference with the rest of us is that their maps are more comprehensive, and they are aware that all systems of thought, all explanations, and all perspectives, are only pointers to the truth and are made up by human beings. Therefore, incomplete and approximate. And since the wise know this, they are not attached to their current views, but are willing to modify them as they progress.

The road to wisdom must start somewhere, and people frequently have difficulty finding out what works and what wastes time. Especially nowadays, when we have an overdose of information, an overwhelming number of choices, and little discernment on what to choose.

Starting a spiritual journey does not entail selling your belongings, breaking up your existing relationship, or quitting your job. It does not mean you either engage in religion or live in an ashram in India. Most people start with the awareness that they have followed the signposts given by society and achieved the right goals, yet they do not feel the satisfaction they expected. Others face an enormous crisis that cannot be solved or overcome in the same manner they were used to, so they begin searching elsewhere. Some people realize they cannot quench their thirst with what is presented to them by their environment. Others keep asking themselves profound questions for which society does not provide satisfying answers... In all cases, one realizes that things are to be revealed beyond the veil of a previous reality. But the person does not know how to begin unraveling the web he or she is entangled in. In any event, it does take a certain amount of effort and commitment to inner work. Effortlessness always breeds meaninglessness, so we will not develop much if we do not proactively move forward.

We will include methods of self-improvement, using the term broadly, ranging from psychotherapy, to volunteering, to diving into contemplative practices, aiming at finding our essence, higher consciousness, and higher potential.

Besides what we have been talking about already, here we will present some guidelines that can give direction to start our own path of growth.

1. Counseling, psychotherapy, and bodywork

Everyone has some level of disease in the body, mind, and in the emotional and energy fields that need healing. Whether we admit it or not, experiences leave us with wounds. If we do not cicatrize them, we are bound to keep suffering from them in obvious and mysterious ways: situations that keep showing up in our lives, all sorts of neuroses, different kinds of psychosomatic illnesses, self-sabotaging behaviors, harming and toxic relationships we find ourselves in, past fixations that we are unable to overcome, fears that we cannot face and that are crippling us... Therefore, it is advisable to consider past injuries, overall patterns, chronic issues, mental debris, core false beliefs we have been feeding, and recurrent feelings of dragging our feet. To resolve the underlying problems that represent obstacles to our progress, we must open up to explore the past and its impact on our present. Since both are intimately connected, this must be tackled in our mind and in our body.

We all need psychological support, holistic healing that includes bodywork, and guidance in unraveling dysfunctional patterns to allow for expansion into our whole and resplendent essence. Many aspects of ourselves have been relegated to our subconscious mind because they were too painful to deal with at the time. There are wounds we were never able to heal, although we may have even forgotten about them already. There may be shame, guilt, or fears that keep haunting us because they are buried in our "shadow" (as Carl Jung used to call it).

It is damaging us today because we cannot integrate it into our personality and life in a healthy fashion. More often than not, we require external help and expertise to act as a mirror of what we can no longer see. A trained therapist can help us disentangle our knots, put order in our psychological mess, restore our health, balance our energy, and give us the courage to face what we have been trying to avoid for too long and without positive results. Avoidance is never the solution. Our path of evolution to higher stages will be jeopardized if we do not dig and clean up our memories, release pain and fears, and work on our flaws and weaknesses.

It is also handy to gradually dismantle our defensive personality structure through psychological inquiry and therapy. By exploring, understanding, and dissolving all of our false self-images, clearing out our shadows, and facing our distorted projections, we can ensure that our base is firm instead of having a muddy one that will engulf us as soon as we think we are reaching any summit. It is necessary to work with yourself first before going on any quests to help others or aid the planet.

2. Delving into inner knowledge

Inner development is crucial for wisdom. It is about seeking to understand who you really are, exploring your identity, and pursuing a relentless search for yourself. Only those who believe it is possible to grow beyond the psychological independence of adulthood continue to expand their knowledge to get closer to a "self-transforming mind," as Robert Kegan calls it.

Socrates' proclamation was "Know thyself." Self-knowledge requires more than intellectual self-examination. It demands knowing something about your feelings. The more attention you pay to your emotions and the workings of your mind, the better you will understand why you do the things you do. The more you know about your habits, the easier it is to improve them.

We have to question ourselves: Who am I? Who do I want to become? Where am I? Where do I want to go in this lifetime? Am I aware of the different dimensions of myself? What blocks me from progressing? Why is my life the way it is? Why do I make choices that damage me? Why am I feeling trapped?

All questions that we may have about life arise from this one fundamental question: Who am I? Of course, there is no stable answer, as it changes with time and a rise in consciousness. But certainly, self-examination is a first step that should push us to question every aspect of our approach, including our methodology, biases, and deeply held assumptions.

Self-reflection is the key to having a real and profound change within ourselves. Without sufficient awareness, attempts to change oneself by imposing different behavior cannot sustain lasting results. Knowing ourselves directly affects outcomes in our life and our ability to respond to life's circumstances with courage, lucidity, and determination.

This psychologically nuanced introspection requires that we honestly challenge our beliefs and dare to act on the information we gain, which may lead to fresh ways of thinking about our lives and our goals. We must look at our relationships, values, how we spend our time and resources, and respond to other people and situations more broadly. We must regularly review our motivation, behavior, and objectives to advance our inner development. It is not about self-absorption and overthinking but about knowing who we are right now to become who we can be. And that knowledge must help us take charge of our life.

We will acknowledge that we are not perfect or a finished version of the person we may become, yet we will support ourselves through thick and thin, showing self-compassion instead of destructive criticism. Approval from outside sources can be encouraging, but we must approve of ourselves the way we are. It cannot be contingent on any accomplishments. Each of us is a work in progress. And at the same time, totally worthwhile and valuable right now. This is how we become empowered. Without this confidence, all progress will be frustrated by a lack of self-esteem, making us dependent on others' admiration and acceptance.

3. Exposing ourselves to a variety of life experiences

Research has shown evidence for certain facilitating conditions for developing wisdom, such as challenging and stressful life events, because they force us to change, resulting in a greater tolerance for uncertainty, fewer projection tendencies, greater resilience and humility, and less self-centeredness. Positive experiences may also facilitate wisdom by fostering integration and coherence with our values. Being able to go through many changes opens up many doors and allows for many beginnings, allowing us to develop patience and flexibility. As Stephen Covey said: "Just as we develop our physical muscles through overcoming opposition—such as lifting weights—we develop our character muscles by overcoming challenges and adversity."

We learn the most from the challenges that test our boundaries, resistance, and awareness on every level. When these experiences arrive, they push us out of balance and can lead to helpful reflection and searching. They can also help us identify some obstacles or weaknesses inside of us. If we can turn the hurdles into learning opportunities, we can have greater possibilities to keep growing instead of looking for the comfortable cubicle that makes us feel in control.

Traveling extensively and being in touch with other cultures expands our views as we realize that our perspectives and beliefs are only some out of the many ones available, not necessarily the best. We recognize that many opinions we hold dear are formed through the media or other people's beliefs that we have taken as truths. Traveling can make you question many of these, and in addition, you learn about yourself. Exposure to surprises and the unexpected when you leave home forces you to work on your versatility and open-mindedness, especially if you go to foreign countries. This is less likely to happen if you never leave your routine and the safety net of people similar to you.

Besides, we tend to take for granted our blessings, and we usually do not fully realize that many individuals on this planet will never have or enjoy many things we accept as usual. Going to poorer places helps us put our life into perspective and allows us to recognize the importance of just the basics.

Of course, traveling alone can multiply the benefits mentioned above since you are obliged to mingle more with locals and new fellow travelers, and you have no guide to take you by the hand or a group to lean upon. You must develop confidence, communication, curiosity, fortitude, and so on. You expand your risk tolerance, feel at ease with yourself, become comfortable with long periods of silence, explore your mind, increase your level of mindfulness and attention, face difficulties, and rely on yourself... It can indeed be a transformational experience in itself.

4. Studying inspirational and sacred teachings

It is too easy to get absorbed in daily life, to be concerned only with the logistics of life and the repetitive motions we must carry out every day, responding to the many material responsibilities we have. This leaves no time or space for our inner development, our most critical task.

Fortunately, we live in an era with plenty of resources that can guide us. Regular study of inspirational books and texts can be a good reminder, foster our spiritual practice, and help us move forward. This can be done with the support of a group (generally more needed by extroverts) or alone (the preferred choice for introverts).

To progress on a spiritual path, it is crucial to work on oneself consciously. In our world today, full of futile distractions and endless to-do lists, it is natural to get sidetracked despite our good intentions.

We are not talking about studying tradition, dogmas, or accepted religious scriptures, but more about working with spiritual or sacred books that will lead us to cultivate higher ideals and qualities we are all born with. These seeds of light must be regularly fed, watered, and taken care of, or else they will never grow into the tree of virtue and enlightenment we are called to become.

Therefore, it is crucial to set aside time to read and study teachings that can help us understand the depth and truth taught to humanity from the most ancient times. According to our personal situation and level of comprehension, we can adjust the inspirational texts we read to each stage.

We should also make specific plans to put into practice what is understood and, from time to time, review whether we are experiencing signs of progress. It is useless to become highly theoretical and entangled in concepts, risking getting lost in theological philosophy and discussions that do not lead to developing inner heart qualities. Philosopher Sri Shankaracharya expressed it this way: "The web of words is a great forest that causes the mind to wander and creates confusion." Let's not forget that knowledge must lead to wisdom through practice and integration of experience.

5. Volunteering

Working altruistically for others, giving back to the community, helping the downtrodden, exchanging your place with others less fortunate, and providing a hand to people who are sick, lonely, or forgotten by the world are all very valid approaches to feeling through your own experience how others feel, as you walk — even if it is just for a little while — in other people's shoes. It is no longer a story you may have heard, a documentary on television, or a belief of another. It is something you experience for yourself and stays with you forever.

Volunteering allows you to step out of your bubble, your petty worries, your tendency to complain, your well-known environment, and your familiar views, and turn into something very different. It gives you a chance to see other people's lives first-hand and to practice giving to others who are not connected to you by blood or friendship and those who cannot pay you back.

It is an excellent way of cultivating unconditional love for all sentient beings and genuinely feeling that no matter how far, how different, and how poor others are, they are human beings just like you. I must admit that I only began to deeply feel that I belonged to one human family when I volunteered in Africa at an orphanage and a school; when I shared some of my time with patients who had no visitors in a hospital and with children who were very sick with cancer; when I lived in a cottage with a Thai family; when the Philippine tribe Aeta took me in for a few days in their remote village; when I slept at the shanty place of a prostitute in South East Asia... Before that, I knew we were all interrelated, but it was more of a theoretical concept than a reality permanently rooted in me.

It is crucial to increase your sense of justice and fairness and to feel concerned by other people's destinies. It makes you more respectful of others' work, condition, and fate. It makes you more humble and compassionate because you really know what it is like to suffer more than you could have ever imagined. It also helps to overcome the sense of hopelessness and disenchantment with the world by contributing. Ultimately, it allows you to feel the oneness of all humans on this planet, which is the basis of the highest development of consciousness.

6. Developing integrity

Eleanor Roosevelt used to say: "One's philosophy is not best expressed in words; it is expressed in the choices one makes... and the choices we make are ultimately our responsibility." There is a time in everybody's path when one realizes that the ego has to surrender its will and ambitions to the common good. At that point, the motivation changes. The person becomes aware of the need to lead an ethical life with heightened self-discipline, minimum emotional conflict, and an all-encompassing compassion for all living beings. This is a necessary passport to travel to higher realms.

Ralph Waldo Emerson wrote: "Sow a thought, reap an act; sow an act, reap a habit; sow a habit, reap a character; sow a character, reap a destiny." The foundation of a good character is a virtuous mind. Virtue consists not in resisting evil but in not even wanting it. Integrity comes when the mind and the heart are aligned. Therefore, it is not just an external behavior; it is mainly a solid decision to remain true to yourself and the ethical principles that you believe in and that are beneficial to all.

One of the most challenging things is to remain balanced and unaffected by criticism or praise since people cannot know you as you really are. We live in a complicated world with plenty of traps that make us fall into lower states of consciousness, eventually leading to more suffering. It takes a strong character and outstanding commitment to only do wholesome actions and to see through the allure that seduces the ego. Instead, we should act from a place of inner discipline, honesty, lucidity, and serenity.

Integrity helps you take appropriate action and occasionally no action at all. It requires a strength of will and character that we generally have to work on. It means that somehow you have identified with the highest level of needs or desires in the hierarchy without deceiving yourself when they conflict with other desires or when the ego craves immediate gratification in the form of an argument, becoming aggressive, or getting something even if that will hurt another. Integrity is a good judgment of what is worth doing, a willingness to do what is fair, and a responsibility to ethical principles, even when it is not the easiest choice.

One cannot open the doors of inner peace and spiritual experiences without building a solid base of kindness and moral values. Temptations and tests abound along the road, and it is imperative to have clear lines of intention and behavior, so you are not bent toward manipulation or corruption, depending on which way the wind blows. Inner integrity has to be above all circumstances, regardless of a changing environment, possible peer pressure, or subtle fears. Having integrity means that we will follow through on our commitments to kindness and ethics, no matter what.

7. Going beyond ego-centeredness

Most people live their whole lives focused on their immediate concerns: ego achievements and how situations and others can be of use or a threat to themselves. They cannot contemplate the interconnectedness of all things, the existing complementary perspectives, the long-term consequences of their actions, or the importance of being beneficial to others.

All the main spiritual traditions affirm that the ego is the greatest obstacle to our higher evolution, personally and culturally. It is funny to realize that what is considered successful in our society is what these traditions consider very destructive to the evolving soul: greed, lust, and vanity. In that sense, it is challenging to go against the tide of our culture. Nothing around us supports the notion of unity and the need to dissolve the ego to swim in the ocean of oneness. We live on such a superficial and limited sensory-based level of experience that we forget that our essence of being is deeply hidden within. Yet, to progress on our spiritual path, we must step out of the cave of ego-centeredness, narcissism, and self-gratification. It does not mean we will not be kind and caring to ourselves—far from it. We will stop taking everything so personally and become less obsessed with our own persona.

Leaving the ego aside requires the willingness to be instructed, the willingness to learn, and the willingness to revise or unlearn things that have proven to be counterproductive for us. It requires restraint. It also requires that we hold in abeyance many of our most primal and compulsive needs—the need for recognition, the need for validation, the need to be the center of the world, the need to be accepted by others, the need to win, the need to be unique, special and even superior, and the need to have all of our wishes fulfilled. Tennessee Williams stated:

Nobody sees anybody truly, but all through the flaws of their egos. That is the way we all see each other in life. Vanity, fear, desire, and competition—distortions within our egos—condition our vision of those concerning us. Add to those distortions to our own egos the corresponding distortions in the egos of others, and you see how cloudy the glass must become through which we look at each other.

If we cannot go beyond our ego, we will keep repeating the same scenarios and playing the same roles over and over without any chance to escape *samsara* and find the realm of peace, fulfillment, and love that we can see right here, right now.

8. Work on humility

I once heard a saying: "The door to the kingdom of God is exactly as high as you are when you walk on your knees. If you are standing tall, full of pride, you cannot get through." I find this so true.

Recently, I attended an international meeting with a few speakers. The Dalai Lama was there, and also some Western thinkers. It was pretty surprising to witness how most of those thinkers felt so distinguished that they would not bow in respect even an inch when greeting him. Right there, it made me reflect on the great value of humility and how only the most evolved ones have integrated this virtue. The rest still think it is a sign of weakness—nothing could be farther from the truth. Only wise people can recognize that the more you progress, the more you become an instrument of something greater. Therefore, you must dilute your self-importance to hold the light this world desperately needs. If you use it to brighten your ego, you are wasting your gifts and are trapped in your own delusions of grandeur. If you use it to blind others, flashing it in their eyes, it is useless.

Of course, this is very challenging in our contemporary culture, where the opposite behavior is promoted. We are brainwashed about how you have to get ahead by tirelessly promoting yourself, taking center stage, impressing others all the time, selling how awesome you are, and claiming as much credit as possible, even if this means climbing on the backs of others, criticizing people, or despising them.

Humility has nothing to do with low self-esteem. On the contrary, in humble people their self-esteem is not attached to their personal traits, physical appearance, wealth, shortcomings, possessions, or past. Instead, it is related to their unique purpose in life and the empowerment to fulfill that purpose for the common good. They do not compare themselves or feel in competition with others. They relate to others on the same level without any need to show off, raise admiration, or impress them. They treat everyone in the same manner, kings and beggars, because they know these are just human beings with the same struggles and aspirations of happiness as them, and they are equally on the same difficult path toward inner advancement (whether they are aware of it themselves or not).

Therefore, the search for meaning and significance should not be confused with personal ambitions for worldly success or pride. From a spiritual perspective, humility should be cultivated, as the meaning of one's life is intimately related to serving a greater purpose: to contribute in whichever manner we can to others' happiness.

It is therefore fundamental not to take ourselves too seriously, nor to take full credit for our accomplishments (since we know that a big part is due to different causes and others' support). An excellent example of this occurred after World War II. In response to all the accolades that came his way, Winston Churchill humbly commented: "I was not the lion, but it fell to me to give the lion's roar."

9. Appreciating the difference between conventional reality and ultimate reality

People who have embraced the universal wisdom perspective in traditions such as Vedanta, Mahayana Buddhism, or the perennial philosophy indicate that existence involves two different kinds of reality.

i) **The conventional reality** involves our everyday experience and understanding of how the phenomenal world appears and functions. It believes that everything is separate, solid, and has its existence, separate from everything else. This is what most of us mistakenly take as the only reality.

ii) **The ultimate reality.** Beyond our concepts, analysis, and duality lies an eternal truth with no distinctions or separation. A boundless, pure, and perfect ground that enables oneness, the realization of our deepest Self. This is a direct experience of the ultimate truth, selflessness, or emptiness that lies beyond duality.

It is essential to understand this distinction in order to integrate it and use it on our development path. We must remember that "emptiness" (as used here) does not refer to nothingness or some nihilistic view. Emptiness refers to our daily experience and perception of the world and ourselves as unreal. It is currently empty of the qualities and attractiveness we usually assign to it. This is undoubtedly difficult to explain with words, as we are referring to something beyond conceptualization. It is a perception that hides behind that. Only by directly experiencing selflessness can we end the confused projection of our ego and its lack of the external world and people.

We need to live and act in the conventional reality, where we apply common sense and try to find successful practices to survive, overcome suffering, and thrive. However, we should also realize that beyond this experience that we share on Earth, there is the infinite, the permanent unity, the eternal, the never-ending love that is our true nature.

There is no contradiction here. There is no true-false dichotomy. Absolute and relative are not separate. As it is written in the Heart Sutra: "Form is no other than emptiness; emptiness no other than form. Form is exactly emptiness; emptiness exactly form." This is the paradox to be integrated: the

Absolute is related to the relative, and the relative is associated with the Absolute. Together, they make up reality.

In other words, we are material and spiritual at the same time. We have a body and a mind, but we are not our body and mind. We are the energy in constant flux that cannot be destroyed, just transformed. We live a life with a beginning and an end, but the consciousness that ignites life existed before and will exist afterward. We may appear separate and distinct, but that is only part of the illusion we must overcome in order to develop.

I like using a simple metaphor to facilitate understanding. When we come to this planet, we have a role to play in this theater called life. We enroll with some script, aware of certain events and people we will encounter. We have yet to determine how we will act then, although we may have a clear idea beforehand of how we should. Once incarnated, we no longer remember our good intentions and plans. We become so involved and identified with the role we agreed to play that we think we are the role, and so the show becomes a drama we are totally ensnared by, forgetting the big picture. However, at some point, the play is over for us, the game ends, and we leave all that seemed important behind. It is then that we realize again that we come as visitors here for a short time. We suddenly recall the initial design we participated in and the fact that we are the actors, not the role we were playing for a little while. Understanding the existence of both conventional and ultimate reality can help us be aware of this now, without the need to wait for our physical death.

Chapter 16

How to reach graduation

We are also players upon a stage. The stage changes. The acts ring down. The lights come up once again.

And throughout the grand illusion and the following and the following there is the undergirding majesty of the One Infinite Creator. All is well. Nothing is lost.

Ra, *The Law of One*

Many say: "I am a good person, and I believe in God, so I am certain I am prepared to ascend." It is not that simple. Human beings are divine sparks, so we have the potential for the perfect Divinity. We have an inherent tendency to be good people. This does not mean that we are going to move up immediately. It requires crucial inner work because evolution is done from the consciousness of who we are and progressing from the ego to the Higher Self. Therefore, it is not achieved only by being a good person.

Let's realize that we are approaching what *The Law of One* calls "the harvest," which I prefer to call "graduation" because it is much easier to understand. We have gone through many cycles of incarnations that have allowed us to experience matter and duality on this low-vibration planet. This allows us to learn and take back so many experiences to Source. Everything that has happened to us has a reason, although we could not understand it at the time. Our soul has chosen the most appropriate encounters and circumstances for our growth. Everything has been perfect as it was. We have had countless opportunities to develop our wisdom and compassion. We have been through plenty of classes and training. And now, we are in the middle of the intense final course before passing the last exams, because the time for graduation is around the corner.

Similarly, not everyone will be able to graduate when finishing college. Some will have to repeat several subjects, and others entire courses. The graduation speed is not imposed from the outside, as we have the free will to decide our learning pace. Everything in the Universe is done with great care toward each of us. There is nothing random. Everything is full of unconditional love. Therefore, the keys I give below can only be helpful for those interested in graduating. If you are reading this book, I assume that you are.

1. The first key is RESPECT

We must learn to truly respect those who are different from us, the ones who have made other choices, the ones who prefer to remain hooked on the Matrix, the ones whom we perceive to be on the wrong path, and even the ones who allow themselves to be dominated. Everyone has sovereignty over their life, even if it is a family member or a close friend. Of course, we would like everyone to make the same decision and be able to walk the same path together. The reality is that it does not work that way.

It is our prerogative to choose how we live our life and make decisions about our mind, our body, and the use of our vital energy. This does not make us better or worse than anyone else, just sovereign. You have to respect others the way you want to be respected.

We are not gods with the capacity to perceive the grand plan of every soul. We do not know the causes and conditions each soul has selected, their karma, or the lessons they must go through. Furthermore, we have yet to learn about the experiences they have picked to experience. Setting ourselves up as judges is improper. Even taking on the role of savior is not correct. We are not here to convince anyone of anything, no matter how passionate we are about our cause or perspective. All roads lead to Rome. Some are more direct, others run through hills, and others take detours. Ours is not the only one, nor should we generalize it. It is perfect for us, but we can't necessarily extrapolate to everyone else. Every path is sacred.

The opposite of respect is judgment, which is prevalent among human beings. Believing that we have the truth is a common characteristic of the ego because it infuses itself with a very effective layer of superiority. Like peacocks, it allows us to show (or perceive) ourselves as inflated and shiny. It is a ploy that makes us sink and disconnects us from consciousness. It separates us from our brothers and sisters, pits us against them, and destroys us. Vilifying others and judging them under any excuse is unacceptable and delays our spiritual awakening. It is a significant obstacle.

2. The second key is BALANCE

It is difficult to find balance when our life is full of obligations and activities, and lived at a hasty pace. It is virtually impossible if we are nervous, stressed, or worried. Similarly, if our head is a symphony of noise, chaos, and cacophony, any message received or any disagreement becomes a drama or a threat to our fragile stability. Such a life is perceived as a walk on a tightrope, or a Ferris wheel from which we can never get off. Thus, we cannot pretend to move on to another stage of evolution.

Being in balance means staying anchored, no matter what happens. We are talking about mastering the ability to remain on our axis even if there is conflict or confusion around us. It is achieved by cultivating patience and temperance rather than reacting angrily and automatically. Keeping neutral is one way to avoid getting onto a merry-go-round of feelings. If our partner makes a lousy gesture or gets angry, do not get mad. If colleagues gossip about others, do not be drawn into these bad vibrations. If the child throws a tantrum, do not allow him to lose it. If we are threatened with draconian measures, we do not fall off a cliff of panic.

It is about operating with equanimity, mental clarity, and inner silence to choose rather than be dragged. Like a mountain firmly settled on the solid ground of nature, watching the seasons, the storms, and the winds pass by without feeling personally involved. You understand that everything is ephemeral. Nothing can cause unease, anger, or anguish in us without our permission. Knowing that you are responsible for your mind, you can accept what comes with simplicity and without resistance. Reactivity is no longer a tolerable option. People and their circumstances matter to you, but you recognize that their suffering is not up to you, nor is it under your control.

By taking on the role of the witness, you can observe everything carefully. Still, you do not allow external circumstances to determine your emotions, feelings, and thoughts, living on a constant rollercoaster. Otherwise, we will not be prepared to climb to the fifth dimension since it requires total mastery over emotions, owning our mind, and remaining with inner peace at all times. It is essential to move from an external to an internal modus operandi.

3. The third key is DETACHMENT

Here, we are talking about all kinds of attachments, the material ones. If we are clinging to our house, car, money in the bank, or possessions or properties, that will prevent us from changing. And what is coming is not just a change but a fundamental transformation. That feeling of not wanting to lose what has been achieved or accumulated because it took us effort or time to get there does not justify grasping. Rationalizing attachment does not dissolve it; it only strengthens it.

There are many more types of attachments to overcome to move on to the next phase. To all the events that happened and hurt us, to the mistakes that we made and still weigh on us, to the battles that we did not win, to the dreams that we could not turn into reality, to those who are no longer in our lives... None of that has any relevance in the present. We can only take away the lessons learned. The rest are weights that will prevent us from flying.

Another critical detachment to manage relates to beliefs, opinions, and other mental scaffolding we have created. This starts from the basis that we have been subjected to programming from a very young age to accept the rules of the game of duality through our family, society, and culture. Many of us see that we have also been taught to think in a certain way that benefits the people in power and keeps us from being who we really are. In other words, many of our beliefs are determined by external forces shared by thousands or millions of people, but this does not make them indisputable truths. They are simply dictated by so-called authorities or experts who convince you about how you should think, feel, and act. Any kind of questioning is perceived as a threat to the system and even to most people who have internalized that way of thinking.

Upon waking up, we must question each dogma we have received. Albeit, they were pillars on which we built our certainties. No belief is sacred or solid. Everything has to be examined, and we must maintain sufficient open-mindedness to review everything we have been told. They are merely suppositions, even if they are covered in layers of plausibility and supported by numerous scientific studies.

We have now learned that many alleged experts have been corrupted by the highest bidder. Although what we have been given may seem credible, it does not mean it is true.

We are beginning another era, the age of awakening. That, in essence, is searching for the truth, questioning what is commonly accepted, investigating rather than following mass media propaganda, rethinking previous certainties, and making yourself responsible for your life without waiting for others to tell you what to do. Submission is obsolete. Nobody should dictate how you think or behave to be a good citizen who blindly follows the herd.

Finally, I would like to add detachment from expectations. It is important to remember that graduation is an individual process and that not everyone will be ready for the final exam immediately. Some people will need more time and extra lessons to do well on the test. Insisting that we predetermine future steps will only frustrate us. When we see that things turn out to be different, we will create useless suffering that will block our way.

We are unaware of what each soul's plan is like, not even ours. We do not know how the next chapter will develop, although we may have some notions about it. Not only that, but we cannot even imagine how wonderful it is to live enlightened, having transcended the limiting veils of duality. If we insist that things be a certain way, we will waste our energy on useless mental fantasies.

4. The fourth key is not to live FROM THE EGO

The next call urges us to act from the Higher Self, leaving aside the familiar tricks and manipulations of the ego. We must stop identifying with the personality. Constant self-observation is essential to achieve this at all times when we are aware of it, for example when we are being provoked and do not respond in the same way; when we try to be the center of attention; when we want to feel above others; when we compete to feel special, or argue to be on top and right; when we project our weaknesses onto others instead of looking at ourselves and trying to overcome them; when we lie to and trick others in our eagerness to stand out or take advantage, and so on.

The ego adopts multiple disguises, and in doing so, we deceive ourselves by justifying ourselves and stumbling on the same stones repeatedly. When we point out and judge others instead of respecting their idiosyncrasies, it is the ego wanting to put itself in the role of the virtuous one. When we criticize what we consider to be the faults of others or give uncalled-for opinions, we overlook the fact that everyone acts to the best of their ability. More often than not, it is wise to keep our free ideas to ourselves or, even better, shift them into compassion for the other person, transmuting the hostile stare into something more constructive.

The ego always seeks to dominate or be dominated, to have power over others, or to feel victimized by circumstances. Its favorite thing to do is to mind other people's business rather than working on one's weaknesses or admitting an inferiority complex. Disidentifying oneself from this tiresome ego in a perpetual state of helplessness is one of the most extraordinary tasks that we—third-dimensional humans—have to complete.

Having confirmed that the ego is never a good counselor or boss, ascension implies that the center of gravity is placed in the Higher Self instead. The ego must be transcended to not give in to *Homo sapiens'* survival impulses, as we are called to become *Homo Christus*. That entails freeing oneself from the chains of instincts and living every moment from consciousness.

Justifying that we are mere animals on two legs to excuse our behaviors is no longer valid. We are Starseeds—spiritual beings who forget our origins to immerse ourselves in this material and dual vibration for a while. We came to gather information and experiences with which to enrich the Whole. The next phase has arrived for those who wish to participate. It is time to start living meaningfully. It is time to wake up from our lethargy. Furthermore, it is time to align ourselves with our essence.

In this new era we are inaugurating, coordinates can no longer be based on ego, individuality, conflict, confrontation, power, wealth, and recognition. They must be rooted in cooperation, unity, interconnectedness, brotherhood, peace, harmony, beauty, and goodness. This is the vetting process of moving from the ego to consciousness, and we must carry it out in our daily lives so that it is not only a beautiful idea but a proven fact.

5. The fifth key is to use our CREATIVE POWER wisely

Even though we are now in a human vessel and barely have access to our ancestral and multidimensional memory, we are divine beings. Our divinity allows us to create through our thoughts and emotions, although we are unaware of it. That is why we must be flawless in our use of mind and speech, for the consequences of our actions manifest themselves outside, both negatively and positively.

We have a great responsibility, and we cannot allow ourselves to continue with the twisted habit of doing things well and ethically only when in others' presence or when trying to duck out. Nor by cheating at the expense of the wellbeing of others. It is inappropriate to behave like rogues, crooks, and narcissists who act out of self-interest. Such behaviors, misaligned with the common good, and lacking empathy and integrity, only remain in the third dimension. It is here where most people still act from the program of biological survival. Without being consistent with higher principles, the results of our creation are poisonous to both the individual and the collective—something utterly unacceptable in more evolved planes of consciousness.

The most creative people—those in contact with the collective unconscious or the subtlest worlds—use inspiration to create art, books, or various inventions. Imagination can also be a means of creation, as it helps us access the resources of the brain's right hemisphere instead of relying solely on the rationality and analysis of the left hemisphere. This is not easy in a society that enhances only what is logical and verifiable. Yet, it is possible and advisable. The system certainly does not make that any easier. Political and religious powers have never welcomed inspiration or free and individual access to information. Everything that escapes from the control network is persecuted and denigrated in one way or another. It does represent a challenge to authority. The intention is to make us believe that we are insignificant and ignorant beings who must be told what to think, how to behave, and how to live our lives. Enclosed in a fold, we are not dangerous to the powers that be. The problem is that we have believed it.

We are indeed powerful beings. Our divine origin allows us an uninterrupted connection with the creator of our universe. Being their fractals gives us a unique creative ability. As a result, whether we know it or not, we are continually creating, and our life is our most outstanding work.

In this dimension, the manifestation of our fruits is usually not so immediate. That is why we tend not to relate them to our own doing. We often do it unconsciously, not knowing that we are carrying it out. That is why we need to look at what we have in our subconscious mind, our shadows, and our deepest beliefs because they are the source of what we bring out in the world. Hence, the impeccable use of thoughts, words, and emotions is necessary to ascend since our vibration increases and our ability to create becomes more evident and faster. If we are not entirely aligned with honesty, integrity, and balance, we could display a horrifying world in record time. That would be unacceptable.

However, those who master the Matrix know the existence of this tool in us perfectly. It is used and enhanced on numerous occasions through fear, for instance. People who feel threatened or think about future scary scenarios create those things without knowing it. Solid and vivid emotions go a long way in making something feel more real, infusing it with the powerful energy required for manifestation. That is why it is critical to master our emotional fluctuations and be absolute owners. If we are still susceptible to external triggers that push us out of our center, we cannot move to a stage of higher consciousness in which creation is accelerated. Without reaching a developed degree of neutrality, compassion, and equanimity, our infinite potential would be completely uncontrolled and unbridled, causing significant damage around us.

Part IV

The 5 main keys

Whatever plane our consciousness may be acting in, both we and the things belonging to that plane are, for the time being, our only realities.

As we rise in the scale of development, we perceive that during the stages through which we have passed we mistook shadows for realities. The upward progress of the ego is a series of progressive awakenings, each advance bringing with it the idea that now, at last, we have reached "reality"; but only when we shall have reached the absolute consciousness and blended our own with it, shall we be free from the delusions produced by *maya*.

Helena Petrovna Blavatsky

Chapter 17

Disidentification with the ego

Are you suffering? Ahhh, you must be very attached. Why not let go?

If you let go a little, you'll be a little happy.

If you let go a lot, you'll be a lot happy.

If you let go completely, you'll be completely happy.

Ajahn Chah

In our Western society, everything around us emphasizes and supports an ever-stronger ego or self-identity, so we are conditioned by it since early childhood. We build a separate, limited, defensive self to deal with people and circumstances. This limited self, continuously thinking, feeling, judging, competing, and fearing, is who we are. Furthermore, we have been indoctrinated from a young age to believe that we must always win and that we must always put our own interests ahead of others. The root of this attitude is often fear and feeling lost and alone.

Children fabricate their sense of self by internalizing and identifying with aspects of their parents and how their parents relate to them. The ego identity keeps forming with a collection of images and ideas of oneself that are just mental concepts, not reality. This way, we make our self into something solid, demarcated, and separated from everything else. The main activity of the ego becomes grasping experiences that maintain its perceived identity and rejecting whatever can threaten it. It is desperate to find security and therefore holds on to possessions, justifications, beliefs, and people who seem to provide that.

It is not just a cognitive construction made up of concepts; emotions, primarily destructive ones, also prop it up. When we split ourselves into a self versus another, that self feels fear. As Ken Wilber puts it: "simply because there are now so many others out there that can harm us." If we keep identifying with this tiny and vulnerable self, then others can damage it, insult it, belittle it, and constrain it. The ego is then fed by carrying resentment, anxiety, and dissatisfaction. It actively collects hurts, lacks, secret envies, and hidden desires to reinforce itself and keep growing. It is a self-contraction version of our essence that we are usually completely oblivious to. We sustain it with our habits, such as finding fault with everyone, judging every action and every word, and criticizing others for not being like us or adjusting to our standards. This is actually a serious obstacle to going to the upper scales of wisdom. It is challenging to know what we are doing wrong and what we are doing right when we have so many judgments about what we do. It is necessary to let it go to feel the love and joy present right here and right now for all of us.

We also repeat the old patterns and behaviors we have carefully formed over the years through this carcass called ego, mistaking it for our true self because we are unconscious of its existence. As we are seeing, this very construction is actually the veil that stops us from seeing through it to what lies beyond and keeps us trapped in a composition of elaborated concepts that we identify as ourselves. We feel incomplete because we have been identifying all our life with our thoughts, our feelings, our possessions, our body, our family, our culture, our country, our religion, our political party... Somehow, we have hypnotized ourselves by completely believing our thoughts and other people's suggestions. That way, we keep representing roles with such intensity and drama over the years.

I have always found in the Wachowski brothers' (now sisters') trilogy of movies, *The Matrix*, a great symbol of our planet. At some point in the first movie, the main character— Neo—is given a choice, as he is offered two pills. One will send him back to the life he has known; the other will enable him to explore the truth and enter an alternative world where he will learn about the Matrix. He chooses the latter, which is almost more impressive than he can bear. He then discovers that most people are oblivious and stuck in the collective illusion. As he awakes, he sees that advanced machines create and run the world he considers real.

Every human choice is between waking up or sleeping in the dream of our interpretations, formed by filters, concepts, stories, projections, and false beliefs. To stay hypnotized by believing what we think about what we perceive, continuing to be fixated on these descriptions we have made up individually and collectively. Or to stop this nonsense and experience the world directly. How? By quietening the ongoing dialogue in the mind and living in a realm of silence. Rather than believing that the world around us reflects reality, please recognize that the divine intelligence that orchestrates the universe is beyond our words and theories. Otherwise, the analytical part of our mind takes over, and we lose our opportunity for direct perception.

Our ordinary sense of self is also characterized by a feeling of temporal continuity and sameness over time, a sense of consistency in interpersonal interactions, and others' recognition of this continuity. But the most advanced Eastern psychologies see the ego as unreal and see it as a thick filter that does not let us experience life directly but only through the bias of our concepts, the conclusions we draw from our experiences, the beliefs we adopt, and the strain of our innermost fears— clinging to a sense of personal continuity and self-identity results in chronic discontent and psychic conflict.

The ego is born to be responsible for survival and protection. It is just an operational necessity. According to the ego, we are essentially separate beings, struggling for our own existence, trying to survive, be nourished, and get acknowledgment.

It should just take the role of the security officer. The problem arises when we promote it to the CEO job, as we finally do. Then the ego reckons that it is the sole owner of the business and its goals are the only ones that matter. In this confusion of our true identity lies most of our predicaments. We reduce the vastness of our true nature to a much smaller, simplified version of who we really are. We constrain our essence to a shrunk structure that suffocates us. Not only that, but we mistake the outer façade for the core of our being. We make the ego real and wonder why we are always thirsty, no matter how much we drink.

Metaphorically, we tend to identify with a flower, which blossoms for a short time and then decays and dies. We have forgotten that we are more like a tree with deep roots. We can give fruits to Mother Earth to expand life, which will result in seeds that will grow into trees that are part of us. By bringing life into the world, we are a part of this endless creation and expansion of existence. There is no such thing as death. We are interwoven into a larger field of Consciousness.

The ego serves humans as the instrument for individualization. But once individuality has been formed, believing that we are our ego becomes limiting and harmful, so we have to go beyond its boundaries. That way, it does not become a massive obstacle to our highest development. But, since we took so much trouble building the ego, it is challenging to get beyond it.

The word ego means "I." Without an "I," we cannot be anything in our world. The process of transcending the ego is often misinterpreted as meaning to annihilate or abolish it. On the contrary, transcending it does not mean making it disappear or destroying it. It simply means being without limitations and being able to expand beyond in an integrated manner. It implies including other ways of being. Likewise, it entails not letting the tyrant built through social and cultural conditioning deny the existence of different dimensions of reality apart from those with which it is familiar and comfortable. We need an ego of some sort to deal with the logistics of daily life. As psychologist Jack Engler stated: "You have to be somebody before you can be nobody." You need to be a happy, healthy, well-rounded human before you can go beyond yourself. As we saw in the chapter on spiritual bypass, you need to function well in the world and heal your wounds first before you go into spiritual awakening. Besides, you will always need a functioning ego to carry on daily tasks. As the Dalai Lama said, "You need an ego to get the bus."

We require an ego to deal competently with the physical world of time and space, execution, and strategies. The transpersonal self has to be developed to deal with the psychological world beyond time and space. Both are necessary to live a whole and integrated life. And the ego should always be at the service of the transpersonal. Daily life is not a problem when deluded thoughts and emotions do not trap you. Then you can play by the conventional rules of our society without being absorbed by them. You can live your life and still be aware of whom you extend beyond your limiting beliefs and those of the people around you. You realize that it is all just a game; thus, you are no longer concerned with winning or losing. There is nothing to win or lose. Life becomes a process of experiencing and discovering your true nature. And you willingly embrace it as a path to becoming.

Of course, it all starts by knowing that we are not our feelings. That frees us from their grip, especially when the emotions that arise are destructive, be it fear, pain, or envy. Then we realize that we are the witness, pure consciousness liberated from all emotional and physical states.

However, we must not forget that in the beginning, this is just a mental abstraction, an intellectual understanding, to change our perspective. This in itself does not make our anger or sadness disappear. It just gives us a different path to walk in order not to be carried away by appearances, believing that there is an "I" to defend. For the negative emotions to dissolve, it is important to feel them, sink into them if necessary, and become one with them. It is not by repressing or disowning, or hiding them that they will disappear. They can only dissolve by fully feeling them and then letting them go without feeding them with additional thoughts and images. Otherwise, they sink back into the subconscious mind. Unrecognized feelings will continue to unfold and appear in disguises such as neuroses, sicknesses, lack of energy, or subtle self-sabotage. Telling yourself that you are not feeling them because there is no ego as such will not make them disappear. That kind of trick does not work. We have to be realistic about how to best deal with them. It is critical to face them head-on, whether fear, anxiety, anger, shame, worthlessness, or depression. Contemplative practices teach us that negative emotions do not have to last. It helps when you allow yourself to feel them first, label them, explore their possible cause, and take action (whether physical or verbal or even if the final decision is not to act).

Last but not least, you need to release them completely. You may find that the negative emotion has already disappeared or is morphing into something else after going through this. Regardless, it no longer has a hold on you because you do not consider it part of you, just a passing event in the pristine sky of your mind. That is all.

The ego loves to separate and label. It cannot recognize the underlying unity of all things and beings. Yet, when we go under the level of thoughts, expectations, ideas, and concepts as fabricated by it, we discover our essence as the source of everything we ever need. Only then can we find the everlasting fulfillment we have always sought in the wrong places. There we can finally be bathed in total peace. Our challenge and reward on Earth is to be a unique and individual consciousness and, at the same time, to be connected with the Whole. It is finding out that Home is within ourselves.

When you find peace within, you also notice that you no longer need so many things from the outside world. You free yourself up from any kind of dependencies, and fear disappears. There is no longer any concern that we may not get what we require. There is no longer a fear of losing something we already have. We no longer fear that we lack something or someone that will bring ultimate happiness. We discover we are already everything we could ever need. We inhabit the unchanging spirit that witnesses the games of the ego and its childish behavior with compassion and detachment. We embrace the ups and downs of daily life with understanding and equanimity, knowing that nothing on Earth can be either a threat or a source of long-term satisfaction.

Beyond the contents of the mind, there is a larger and deeper dimension that we hardly notice unless we train ourselves through meditation and stillness. This more extensive and deeper dimension is the presence of non-conceptual awareness, the Consciousness that has no shape, no form, no beginning, and no end. In Tibetan Buddhism, this is represented through the mandala, a symbol of the creative movement of all life forms in the dynamic field of open space. Mandalas are not just simple aids to concentration; they have a much more significant meaning. They portray the way consciousness unfolds, without the need for a central point of self, with no partiality to one's perspective, with an increasing melt of the observer and the perceived. Outside the dualistic view, everything is related at the same level.

As we continuously seek a belief, a person, an idea, an identity, a reaction, or a security to hold on to, we fail to recognize our essential nature underneath. So much movement, distraction, and judgment happens on the surface that we miss what lies in the depths of our being. Our habitual addiction to the grasping tendency of our mind causes us to overlook the core of who we really are. The ego, which believes it is equivalent to the thoughts it has, creates a narrowed sense of self, convinced that it has a limited territory to defend against any competitor and a fragile substance that can be easily injured.

There is only one base for awakening: awareness. That is, honestly, thinking about everything you have been hiding from yourself for years, such as the tendency to judge and criticize, a profound lack of self-confidence, or the fear of being hurt in relationships. It means taking full responsibility for everything you have built, consciously or unconsciously, knowing that it is not part of who you are but can become a mirage that will lead you to a fake oasis.

To begin the path of self-discovery and disentangling the many disguises our ego adopts is to be aware of the subtle mechanisms of the mind and the differences between our role in the world of *samsara* and our true nature. Another approach suggested in previous chapters is meditation, since it helps us to step aside from the incessant flow of thoughts that flood our minds.

Freedom can only be achieved with great determination and perseverance on the inner level. It entails releasing the need for power in every way and realizing our true nature as beings of Light. Although the original function of the ego is to be able to experience itself as a separate entity, we often lose sight of this goal when the illusion of power and control intoxicates us. For the longest time, humans have tried to fill their inner vacuum with power. We believe it could be fulfilled with fighting, dominance, and manipulation. Unfortunately, this only leads to the degeneration of our essence, to attacking our soul's integrity, to a barren land of a total loss of meaning. Power, in fact, is consistently cloaked by ideas that are thought to be good. But it is only a tool of the ego to achieve control. Besides, power is a toxic drug that causes us to lose our minds and lives entirely.

When this feeling has passed, we can connect with a sense of calmness that fulfills every desire because it dissolves them in emptiness. Pure consciousness then becomes an experience that we will not forget. At first, it may just begin with ephemeral glimpses through peak experiences or gaps between thoughts. A silent witness that can act in the world without being confused or carried away by it is what it becomes at the end of the road. This is our destiny as humans. The jewel we are born with is hidden under much coal. This is the perfection we are called to embrace. This is the blossoming that our soul hungers for. All the other things in the world are counterfeits of the real thing. Pure Consciousness is the only real thing that exists. This is what sages, yogis, and mystics throughout the years have called "awakening."

Chapter 18

Compassion

A human being is a part of the whole called by us universe, a part limited in time and space. He experiences himself, his thoughts, and his feelings as something separated from the rest, a kind of optical delusion of his consciousness.

This delusion is a kind of prison for us, restricting us to our personal desires and to affection for a few persons nearest to us.

Our task must be to free ourselves from this prison by widening our circle of compassion to embrace all living creatures and the whole of nature in its beauty.

Albert Einstein

Even if this is not what many self-help gurus say, enlightenment has nothing to do with self-improvement and everything to do with having compassion for others. Compassion is defined as awareness of the pain of others and the desire to relieve it. It is not primarily emotional and dull and is not divorced from wisdom. It is about reaching outside yourself and caring for people you like and dislike, people who deserve your compassion, and those who do not. Furthermore, it needs to be practiced with both victims and perpetrators. Nobody is excluded. Mother Teresa used to say: "If we have no peace, it is because we have forgotten that we belong to each other."

It is said that a feather falling from the wing of a small bird produces a thunderbolt in the far-off worlds since there is an unbreakable bond between all manifestations. We must assimilate our total dependence and interrelation with everything in life. We are all intertwined. Therefore, each thought, word, and action should come with great responsibility. Are we contributing to world peace, or are we creating conflict because there is a permanent battle within us? Are we collaborating with others, or are we competing with them? Are we cultivating kindness or selfishness? Let's remember that cause and effect act continuously and infinitely; thus, we must be careful with our daily motivation.

We can no longer afford to be absorbed in our daily routine, performing our regular chores, caring for our family, and focusing on making money. Once you grow to the highest stages of inner development, other people's predicaments are your business. You cannot pretend that you do not care because they are physically far away, do not belong to your group, or are evil. As long as there is something we can do to address problems in the world, we have to take responsibility.

We do not do it because we are such good people. We do it out of the source of loving-kindness in our hearts that cannot stop itself from expanding to every corner of the world. It is not a virtue of the hands, as generosity can sometimes be understood, or even a quality of the mind to be practiced. It is an endless energy. Once you perceive you are an intrinsic part of it, you tap into it, and then you become only a bridge connecting it to all sentient beings. Once that awareness becomes patent, there is no way you cannot be compassionate. It just flows through you. Consciousness does not fight or reject anything; it simply encircles darkness with awareness.

Most people begin a personal development path out of a crisis that gives them a decisive blow and throws them to the ground. One of the benefits of suffering is that it forces people to do some reflection. When things seem to go well, and life rolls along with our wishes, we tend to become less motivated to deal with the fundamental issues of life. Only when life gets messy and our securities are shattered do we have to face our frustration and suffering and try to find ways to overcome it and possibly make a turn. Through meditation and guided reflection, we can increase our understanding and start dissolving our self-delusions if we commit and make our practice serious. And if the work is steady, we become more sensitive to the suffering of others and attempt to alleviate it.

Being committed to a spiritual path means we closely observe the workings of the ego, an entity others may not know of. So, we are moved to compassion not only by starving children in Africa or immigrants who are fleeing their home country because of war but also by noticing the ways the ego makes us judge others for the way they look or their social status, by projecting our wounds and complexes onto them, by blaming them for our own weaknesses, by believing the stories we make up and tell ourselves. Eventually, we start seeing the many ways self-centeredness harms others. At that point, we realize that we needed to purify ourselves before we could resonate with the truths of ancient wisdom and be of genuine help to others.

Awakening brings awareness of what makes us suffer and brings constant dissatisfaction. By doing so, it also helps us to transcend the bias of the ego. Therefore, perception becomes exceedingly sharp. When we start dissolving the duality of "I" and "you," naturally a "we" emerges. There are no longer two different sides, mine and yours. We are all together in this. Thus, a strong bond is built and shared with other humans, and a stronger sense of compassion is fostered for all living creatures.

A solid foundation of wisdom and insight must be cultivated first because a desire to relieve suffering is not enough. We also have to develop the best tools for achieving it. A selfless nature is crucial to making you potentially helpful to others. If we are still stuck in ego-centeredness, self-importance, and personal ambitions, then our own agenda gets in the way. That is why we have such problems in NGOs and charitable institutions, where greed and corruption pose constant issues for administrators. What begins as wholesome ends up damaging many people involved and diminishing others' trust in institutions that are supposed to be altruistic in nature.

We have numerous examples of people trying to do good but falling prey to selfish interests, which only worsen the conditions of those they are meant to serve. A vicious cycle is created by making the recipients of charity feed the giver's need for self-worth: the givers lessen the self-respect the needy most require in their downtrodden state. This is why working on one's ego entanglements is imperative. It is the best way to ensure that our actions will always be beneficial and not flawed by contrivance. It is the most efficient way to avoid the inherent dangers of applying one's ideals about compassion to real-world situations with mixed motivations from the very beginning.

To progress to the highest stages of wisdom, we must understand that our life has nothing to do with ourselves. It is about everyone whose life we touch and how we touch it. As poet Rumi put it, we must "come out of the circle of time. And into the circle of love."

Being compassionate does not mean meddling in people's lives. It is one thing to have a conversation with someone you appreciate because you believe (and it is just your opinion) that they are going off track, and it is entirely another thing to try to pull them in a direction they do not wish to go. This would be our ego believing that we know better than another what they need. If we were to do that, we would deny their journey and assume that we know the outcome and the lessons to be learned. We would also be denying the value of the experiences and the value of the pathway itself.

To continue with a similar example, we should not infuriate our companion by contradicting, judging, or disrespecting his convictions every time we have a conversation. Instead, it is best to start with their best possibilities, and considering the level of their consciousness, we should gradually and patiently try to broaden their horizon. When we speak kindly, we get rid of every bit of anger and treat the other person like a friend instead of getting annoyed, making fun of them, or putting them down. Only pompous ignorance loves showing off, humiliating, and winning arguments in search of imaginary medals at the expense of the imagined adversary. Therefore, we should manifest mercy and benevolence in every situation.

Compassion goes together with detachment. Therefore, we do not adhere to our vision, judgment, or interference. We leave others free to maneuver. When we are trying to force someone to go a certain way or do a certain thing for their own good, we are being manipulative. That is an ego action that is done neither out of love nor out of prudence.

Compassion entails completely honoring—even without understanding—what someone is going through, whether it is winning a Nobel Prize or dying of cancer. It implies that we deeply respect all choices and experiences. It involves complete trust, not only in the Divine plan but also in the individual's plan. The path is never straight. It goes through many ups and downs, turns, and even round in circles. It does not matter in the long run. In the big scheme of things, it all goes according to the Infinite plan. All strategies and apparent detours are meant to take us to a greater level of wisdom and, ultimately, to enlightenment. That is human destiny. Even if we may not understand or agree with what we consider sidetracks or mistakes occasionally.

As Mahayana Buddhists point out, compassion is a virtue that can and must be developed. If you've never suffered yourself, if you've never seen a child cry in hunger, if you've never seen a mother weep with her dead child in her arms, then compassion is more theoretical.

That is why we should not avoid or try to reject the challenges presented to us. We have to go through tough times to understand better and have empathy for what others go through. Without obstacles, it is too easy to think that we are above it all. We may believe that people deserve what they get, and therefore we should mind our own business, allowing them to wither in their misery and suffering because of their ignorance, as we choose to look aside.

The Dalai Lama represents a great model of compassion. For instance, once, at the end of a stay at a San Francisco hotel, he asked the management to bring out all the employees. This meant the people who chop vegetables in the kitchen, clean the carpets, and make the beds. The big circular driveway became filled with all those who make a hotel work but are usually unrecognized. One by one, he looked at each individual with his entire presence, took each person's hand, and said, "Thank you," moving unhurriedly to ensure that he connected with each one thoroughly. He personifies the power of compassion emanating through presence and actions.

As our level of consciousness increases, we recognize that we are all interconnected and part of a massive chain where the ones ahead willingly help those brothers and sisters who are less advanced, the same way we were assisted by others too. We realize that we are part of the human family and share this planet with other living creatures that, although less evolved, are also companions and are worthy. With our actions and new ways of being, we become examples for others and spiritual teachers. We are aware that we are not isolated entities and do not try to escape from the afflictions of a crazy and immature world. We know that humanity is having problems, and we want to help in any way we can.

We all have the calling to become real Bodhisattvas. These divine beings, worthy of nirvana, remain on the human plane to guide all humanity to ultimate liberation. That is why it makes so much sense that Mahayana Buddhists commit to attaining complete enlightenment for the sake of all sentient beings (the Bodhisattva vow), cultivating supreme moral and spiritual perfection in the service of others. Mainly because that directs our attitude positively, giving us a tremendous impetus in our practice. And in the end, the effect of the vow is to show us how we can become an instrument of help to others in everything we do. As compassion deepens, we develop the nobility of the heart. We can observe how we respond to difficult situations with calmness, clarity, and directness. If we realize that no act of kindness, regardless of how small, is ever wasted if carried out from the heart, we will have a strong sense that everything we do matters. Then, a quiet fearlessness is present, as we no longer fear that we will compromise our own integrity. We also connect with the joy of knowing that every thought, word, and action leaves a trace. Therefore, they are meaningful and can help bring light into the world.

Chapter 19

Seeing perfection in everything

Stop thinking of achievement of any kind. You are complete here, and now; you need absolutely nothing.

Nisargadatta Maharaj

It is difficult to open up to our life experience as it is, when we find that it does not meet our expectations of what it should be. Every so often, we think that we do not fit into the picture we hold of the person we should be. Maybe those we love do not measure up to our ideals. Perhaps we find the state of the world disheartening, shocking, or highly unfair. Reality constantly contradicts our illusions, leaving us with bitterness and a permanent longing that cannot be satiated. We also feel a pervasive sense of dissatisfaction. From that place, it is impossible to find stable serenity. The answer is not to get angry at what we dislike and resist what bothers us. Wisdom is born when we no longer seek an escape and learn to be comfortable with whatever appears at our door.

Real wisdom comes when we see that life is a process of perfection unfolding without a single mistake. Thus, we give up the hope of avoiding the pains and confusions of existence. Awakening is the realization that not only can we not avoid them, but there is also no need to prevent anything from being fulfilled. There is absolutely nothing really blocking us. What appears to be in the way is that we imagine ourselves on the road somewhere, a summit to reach, a feat to achieve. Spiritual awakening does not require a new and better experience. It is simply seeing through our filters without projections, beliefs, or interpretations to appreciate that we already are that, and that we have what it takes. Nothing spectacular, mysterious, or radically different is required.

I have always liked writer Neale Donald Walsh's quote: "When you see the utter perfection in everything—not just those things with which you agree, but (and perhaps, especially) those things with which you disagree—you achieve mastery." And what is enlightenment but attaining the level of mastery as human beings?

We often compromise our capacity to meet experience directly and without the screen of our concepts and expectations—because we want our experience to be different, to change into something better. We typically have inner resistance toward what it is, convinced that it is not enough, that there is a better version elsewhere, that there is always a more complete future, somewhere else to be instead, and another desire to pursue around the corner. There is always something else to chase, another set of actions to take, another object to possess, or another aspect of ourselves to improve before we can finally breathe and be at ease and content in the present. We are convinced that we will only allow ourselves to relax when everything is in order; when we have conquered all the summits; when we have finished all the courses we intended to do; when we have accomplished all the items on our list; when all our dreams come true; when our ideals have been materialized; when nothing is pending.

If we are committed to our soul's evolution, doing cannot be the central theme of our life. The impossibility of stopping this race is because we are busy with so many activities and chores that we do not have time to rest and contemplate. When I speak with participants in my mindfulness courses about this, many promptly point out that they cannot afford the luxury of contemplation because of their constant demands. Some even state that they do not have time for a few daily minutes of meditation. Is this true? Do we really believe that we are getting somewhere wholesome with this behavior? Are we not all buying into a sort of collective delusion? Do we seriously think that we can experience stable wellbeing and balance (let alone awakening) by getting hooked on hectic existences until we die?

Even something as beneficial as psychotherapy can eventually become a hindrance to awakening. Once we work on our subconscious patterns, unhealed wounds, deep fears, and repressed feelings to ensure that we are not using the spiritual path to bypass the less shining aspects of life, keeping focused on constant improvement can reinforce certain tendencies inherent in the personality. We may end up trapped in the misconception that there is always something better to achieve and enhance to get to the next level. That constant obsession with improvement can interfere with a required letting go and surrendering that are fundamental for moving from the personality to the field of being.

The fix mentality only really works on external and physical matters that need a straightforward solution: a broken window needs to be replaced; a sink does not work and you need to change the pipe; the car does not start and you need to renew some parts in the engine... However, if we approach an inner issue in the same manner, it usually has the opposite effect, making us feel rejected or unacceptable, and therefore we tighten up.

It is easy to get lured into endless personal development on the false premise that it will make you a better person, a perfect one. Walking the road toward awakening makes you a more authentic person, more humble, more real, more profound, and more personally involved in the evolution of humanity.

The truth is that there is no way we can get there—to merge with the radiant consciousness—unless we are entirely here (present, cheerful, and content) where we are right now. This is a fundamental step that cannot be avoided.

When we find perfection in everything, then stillness naturally arises. Inner peace can flourish when we abandon our resistance to this precise moment. Then neither the presence nor the absence of any person, place, condition, or situation can affect our state of mind. This does not mean we are never irritated or annoyed, but those feelings do not last and do not get to the core of who we are. We begin to view them as minor nuisances that occur on the surface, in the waves, but we have our consciousness firmly anchored in the ocean's depths. Thus, it does not have the power to distress us. We hold our balance safely inside, where no storm can really impact it.

This does not mean that you have to reject earthly experiences, either. It is just that our involvement with them becomes voluntary, not mandatory. Why? Because we no longer depend on any particular person, circumstance, or object to feel happy, or use anything to justify sadness.

Being can only be revealed in the present moment when analyzing and striving stops. Our concepts of what our reality should look like are usually what stands between us and true fulfillment. Constantly measuring up our standards against what we see becomes a hindrance to experiencing things as they are without believing that something is lacking. Through the lens of our expectations, our living circumstances never lead to contentment because we always want more. What often prevents us from experiencing life in a bare, stripped-down fashion is our thoughts and beliefs about how everything should be and how everyone should behave with us.

We suffer when we think that something is missing from our existence. Since life never follows our rules, this leads us to an eternal dissatisfaction that we try to cover up with more doing, more getting, and more pleasure... Without realizing that, this road only traps us deeper into frustration. Regardless of how much we might achieve, how many people recognize us, how high we get, or how much we possess, our minds will keep telling us that it is not enough. And the saddest thing is that we tend to believe our thoughts instead of questioning them when they bring us distress.

When we allow life to appear as it pleases and when we will enable the experience to show up precisely as it does, without any judgment or resistance on our part, our attention undergoes a significant shift because we no longer need things to be different than they are for us to be happy, fulfilled, and at peace. We do not depend on anything external (or internal) being modified to reach higher ground. We no longer use thinking and thinking as crutches, as well as carrying out more and more duties as a way to escape. Not only that, but we stop trying to climb every available ladder. At that point, we can observe perfection unfolding every second.

There is only one Divine principle—the Absolute—which contains the potentiality of all beings and all creation (therefore, the opposites). It also bears in itself the eternal process of unfolding and perfection. This process is based on the entire system of evolution. Only through perpetual change and integration of opposites can reality be comprehended. Nothing has to be eliminated; everything has a role in the big picture. The universe makes no mistakes. What we get may not align with what we want, but it is precisely what we need. The events of the world reveal a mosaic that can only be perceived from the mountaintop.

Seeing perfection and opportunity in every incident, in every circumstance—no matter how unexpected—in every irritating person we deal with, every obstacle we face, and every sudden turn of events, requires a significant inner transformation. Life brings us what we need on every occasion, even if it sometimes does not appear to be what we want. And when it appears in our life, we take it as if it were our own choice.

This takes a serious commitment, with detachment as well. We have to let go of needs and dependencies of all kinds. We can still have preferences, but when something unexpected happens, something we would not have chosen in the first place, we accept it with grace and without resistance. We give up any sort of inner battle with what we dislike. We relinquish our stories about what is compulsory for us to enjoy wellbeing. We can have plans, but we do not desperately cling to them. We can have a vision, build a path, and act in the world without needing to hide in a cave in the Himalayas. However, we should go with the flow. Not because this is the most spiritual thing to do but because rejecting leads to a dead end and brings great suffering.

It is absurd to fight with what is happening because this is a battle we will lose every single time. Liberation requires us to stop believing that things should be any different than they actually are. It plays to our advantage to go with the current and to collaborate with the universe. It keeps us balanced, alert, and transparent because we do not have to fool ourselves or get distracted to suffer less. Whatever happens is fine with us. Whatever shows up is just a starting point, an opportunity to learn, a stepping stone on our path. Nothing is wrong or inadequate anymore. Nobody has the power to disturb our inner serenity. No circumstance is considered misplaced, because we have assimilated the truth that everything happens for a reason. Events do not happen to us but for us. Every situation, then, is right and indispensable for completing the puzzle of our experience. It is like a mandatory stroke of color on our life canvas. We may not be able to make total sense of the darkest shades at the time, but once the painting is complete, we confirm that it was all fundamental for it to become an outstanding *oeuvre d'art*.

It also means that nothing comes before its time, nothing happens out of place, and therefore nothing will occur that is not meant to. Everything happens at exactly the right moment, with perfect timing, neither too soon nor too late. There is no legitimate judgment to question the perfection of the Infinite plan. The only things we need to keep questioning are our thoughts, biased views of the world, our set ideas about how the world should be, and how people should relate to us to make us feel at peace forever and ever.

We are usually caught up in a bubble, imagining that our feelings, attitudes, and concepts are an accurate portrait of reality. We do not realize that awareness is clouded by unconscious identification with self-images, inner dialogue, conflicting emotions, automatic reactions, and recurring thought patterns. This separates us from fulfillment: being so stuck in the tangled mess of our recurring thoughts and theories about how the world should function and the tricks of the conditioned mind and the personality that we do not allow ourselves to meet the experience with openness and presence. Therefore, we lose it and get lost in the delusions our mind keeps fabricating nonstop. Fortunately, we have the key to leave our old cages and to fly free, soaring into the sky.

There comes a time when you no longer need to decorate the cage so profusely that you forget you are trapped in one. There comes a time when you do not want to acquire gold to paint the iron bars that hold you prisoner, to have the impression of opulence in jail. There comes a time when you can contemplate the game with transparency because you see through the collective illusion, the lies you have been told, and your own mental bias. When you realize that it only takes a change of mindset, a radical transformation of perspective, to step out of the cage and into the absolute infinity of Consciousness, you will see that it is right. Nothing and nobody can hold us prisoners but ourselves.

Given what we just mentioned, we can understand why the possibility of melting in pure Consciousness remains elusive for most of us. As long as we believe there is a goal to be attained by doing something, by changing unattractive aspects of ourselves, by modifying disappointing elements of our life, or by amending errors in our world, it will remain out of our reach. Awakening can only be achieved through being, through anchoring ourselves in the now, where we can connect with a fuller sense of presence, with a powerful feeling of stillness, acceptance, and joy.

Chapter 20

Service: Becoming an instrument of evolution

Lord, make me an instrument of your peace.
Where there is hatred, let me sow love.
Where there is injury, let me sow forgiveness.
Where there is doubt, let me sow faith;
Where there is despair, let me give hope.
Where there is sadness, let me give joy;
O Master, grant that I may not so much seek to receive
compassion as to give compassion.

The Peace Prayer of St. Francis

One of the elements that was crucial on my growth path was the ability to surrender to life. Only after many years of spiritual practice did I reach a point where I was able to accept whatever the universe had planned for me thoroughly. Whatever would come—without resistance, expectations, or whining. It was certainly not easy at all. We are so attached to our ideals and plans that embracing any and every aspect of reality (especially the one showing up that contradicts what you wanted) is very challenging. We try to get things to go our way, pretend that life bends in our direction, and are confident that we know what we need and when we need it. Furthermore, we are so focused on ourselves and our needs and aims that the very idea of dedicating your life to others seems rather far-fetched. Yet, altruism and service are fundamental keys to accessing the highest stages of consciousness.

As Martin Luther King once said: "Everyone can be great because everyone can serve. You don't even have to make your subjects and verbs agree to serve. You only require a heart full of grace." Grace arises when we act with others on behalf of the world.

Service, above all, discloses the path of realization of the common good. No useless rituals, pompous words, or particular beliefs are involved, just cooperation and assistance to humanity. It is an attitude, not a strategy or a religious duty. No expectations are attached. No need for retribution. No waiting for applause. It has to do with the purpose of life, and we must admit that it has a life of its own. A single act of kindness may have a long trajectory and touch those we will never meet or see. It often has a ripple effect since we cannot see the impact of our benevolence. We keep that attitude and way of being because it has become second nature to us. We do not conceive of living, acting, and thinking differently anymore. As Dolores Cannon wrote:

> Humanity is in a place where they require many servers. Not everyone serves in the same capacity or is even aware of it. Many people are unaware of all the lives they have touched by their good work, good words, goodwill, and actions. All people's actions are important.

We are happy to contribute to the beautiful task of spreading peace, compassion, and harmony wherever we are and wherever we go. We agree to become an instrument and give up the idea that we are a captain of other people, an achiever, or someone superior because of some minor achievement. What we offer is who we are, what we have, what we think, and what we do for the benefit of others. We realize that we are a vehicle for something greater than what we could ever become individually and that our job is to purify the channel, so we can contribute to whatever the world needs at each moment. We have no preconceived notions or plans on our part. Somehow we become catalyzers, and we feel that our life does not belong to us anymore, and neither do our individual aspirations and desires. This is not done through sacrifice, pain, or martyrdom. It is done as a natural overflow of the heart, with joy. Let's keep in mind that what really matters is not our doing but our being, the energy we emanate, and the energy we are. It is not what we do but who we are that is the source of fundamental transformation, contrary to what we think. That is why we must reach the upper levels of development. We can be genuinely beneficial if we give up our personal agenda and focus on being a healing presence on this planet.

Experiences either kindle love or sharpen hatred. Who will be the first one to throw a stone? Probably the hater himself. Only working for the benefit of the world will produce the balance we desperately need individually and collectively because it will pour out magnanimity and understanding of Infinity.

You finally understand that great things can be done through you only because you no longer have an agenda of your own. It is not at all forced. It is a more willing renunciation of something you view as useless and childish. Not only that, but it is a spontaneous step on the spiritual path. Unselfishness and benevolence secretly purify the heart and bring peace into the world. Contributing willingly to the Infinite plan is the way to overcome our ego limitations and expand and melt into the One with all.

Offering ourselves to be of benefit means being empty of ourselves (the ego and all the attachments that go with it) to actually serve as a vessel of help, a channel of light in a world of darkness and suffering. Cultivating an unbiased mind and an unconditional love for humanity constitute today the foundation required for a global transformation. The correct action can only be done on this base. Wisdom and courage help us understand the responsibility we have for the welfare of all humanity.

The new humanity will be created by individuals who have modified their motivation, leaving material and egocentric obsessions behind and focusing on benefiting the whole. We are facing a world whose fate is still unsettled. Only by becoming a force for good alone can we build a planet where everyone is considered equal, peace can flourish, every being is seen as worthy, and everyone can live in peace.

An *asana* (position) in yoga, sometimes called "the surrendered warrior," symbolizes the inner movement one needs to make to achieve enlightenment. Giving up and letting go of your plans and individual ambitions is better to assist the collective destiny and humanity's evolution.

Humanity has to go through a transcendent transformation from one level of adolescence (where we are as a species) into adulthood. We are still in progress as a species. We are a work in progress. Thus, we are an unfinished product. But advancement can only be done through real wisdom, which entails understanding and integrating that we are all ONE. We cannot go very far without a commitment to the needs and advancement of our brothers and sisters. Without realizing that our contribution to the whole is of utmost importance, there is no inner development. Without changing our motivation from egocentrism to egolessness, we will find a dead end on our path. We achieve individual evolution when we actively participate in global evolution. There is no shortcut here.

Every heroic, altruistic thought is already a seed for the future world. Not only great masters but every individual can become a builder of good in the world. Every action has consequences, and usually, every effort has multiform results, even if we are blind to them. If we were to witness all the repercussions, we would probably become confused. Only through the broadening of consciousness can one acquire a broader horizon. Even though there is much chaos, there are plenty of injustices, and even though human dignity is being trampled, we can keep our love for humanity and compassion by increasing our level of consciousness.

I am always amazed at the inexhaustible patience and deep compassion of the great masters. Through incalculable eons of time, they have accepted the most oppressive and burdensome incarnations for themselves to move and raise the consciousness of ungrateful humanity, which has persecuted and crucified its liberators and teachers constantly and in every way. I hope that this will change in the coming epoch.

Service is not something forced from the outside. Naturally, you arrive at a point where fighting to push your interest ahead is not relevant anymore. It would be best if you still made a living and were independent. Still, you are no longer obsessed with survival, with the impulses of the body, creating material security, and devising how to use others for your own promotion. Your daily duties and chores still need to be performed, but they do not consume your time or energy. Those commonly shared concerns get dissolved, and you focus on how you can contribute. You should heal and clean yourself first, so you do not stain anything.

The evolution of the universe is like a symphony. In the ongoing concert, there are many instruments. Each one is sacred. Each one has its unique music. Each contributes a particular texture and depth of sound to the symphony. And all of the instruments are playing a shared performance. No device can claim to be the music itself. Each one must bow before the orchestra director and follow his directions. Each one is worthy, and yet not critical, alone and isolated. There is an intimate collaboration of all the musicians because they know that the only thing that matters is the final piece of art. Each one is called to excellence for the sake of all. Each one must play her instrument to the best of her abilities. Each one knows that her work makes sense only within the unity. Each one finds meaning and purpose by contributing to the whole. Nobody pretends to be a solitary star. Every spark adds to the final shine, the magical symphony, and the ultimate masterpiece. This is precisely what we are called to do here on Earth too. Understanding we are just pieces of a puzzle, cells of the same sacred organism, drops of the same ocean, stars in the same constellation. To complete the masterpiece, the universe requires our unique contribution and cooperation. The great mystic Teresa of Ávila expressed it beautifully:

Christ has no body now on earth but yours,
No hands but yours,
No feet but yours.
Yours are the eyes through which to look with Christ's compassion on the world.
Yours are the feet with which he is to go about doing good;
Yours are the hands with which he is to bless men now.

Chapter 21

Being mindful

Do every act of your life as though it were the very last act of your life.

Marcus Aurelius

Wise people are very mindful. They pay attention to whatever may not be working adequately, taking away harmony from their life. Instead of blaming others or external circumstances for problems showing up, they are interested in understanding in depth the roots and opportunities hidden in their development. They do not avoid uncertainty or discomfort since it is part of growing. We are all built to go back to perfection gradually, but the means to get to it and to progress toward transcendence are never direct or without pain.

Humans have inherited a brain system prepared for survival on a planet full of predators and threats that are no longer ours. However, we still feel those intense and strong emotions: fear, anger, hatred, lust, greed, jealousy, craving, envy... all designed to defend us from immediate danger, but which usually get us into great trouble. Unless we train our minds not to fall prey to them and then react automatically in unwholesome ways, we will continue creating much suffering.

We have been conditioned to think that we need to be constantly on the run to control the flow of life and feel proud of our achievements. Thus, we struggle nonstop. It is impossible to feel at peace this way. We feel out of sync with our existence. We cannot connect with our essence or inner stillness and joy. We easily get caught up in the race by trying to find external sources to quench our thirst and calm down our anxiety. This is one of the most significant challenges of our age. The price for controlling reality through thinking and willingness is the nagging feeling of restlessness and damaging stress.

Deep inside, all is well. We can find the peace, harmony, and fulfillment we long for. But we can only access it when we stop thinking, analyzing, worrying, resenting, comparing, and the train of nonstop action. The magical key can only be found in silence and quietness.

On the other hand, as long as we keep emotions at a distance, we are at war with them. We could never keep them outside in the end. They manifest in our body as pains, tension, or perhaps as feeling down or weary. Repressing emotions is not healthy. Observing ourselves is the first step to being liberated from damaging impulses and harmful emotions. As we practice stopping ourselves from seeing our thoughts from the outside, we start keeping some distance from them instead of identifying with everything that our mind fabricates. This can lead to a necessary reflection about the consequences of our actions, the familiar reactions we are hooked on, and the fantasies and delusions we feed, even if we know they are toxic. We can only get the key to change and choose by contemplating ourselves with transparency and honesty. Until we do that, we are just puppets of our past and conditioning. Besides, this allows us to initiate a continuous process of disidentifying with our egoistic ideas, beliefs, concepts, and personality and to stop perceiving ourselves as a separate and isolated entity in a universe full of other independent entities. This way, we become more aware of how we create our own experiences through our thoughts, feelings, and sensations. As we do, we take responsibility for them and discriminate instead of just following our ingrained compulsions. Being balanced, centered, and in a state of clarity allows us to take total responsibility for all our emotions. Ultimately, life is not about being right but about being free and at peace. When we release old emotional responses that have grown into a lifestyle, we liberate ourselves of burdens that no longer belong to us.

We do not realize to what degree we are predictable, bonded to our habits and automatic reactions, programmed by our culture and environment, asleep, and too lazy to care. By rushing everywhere and filling up every minute of our day, we ensure that there is no time to question, no space to center ourselves, and no room for contemplation or silence. We act like sleepwalkers. We keep going as usual. In every aspect of our existence, we assume that more is better. We seem to be caught in a race that leads nowhere. But we keep running, just in case.

Our life carries possibilities and allows us to make choices with these possibilities. The philosopher Heidegger said, "When we fail to face up to our existential condition, we fall back into doing tasks, into mundane inauthenticity." It is crucial to recognize that we are here for a brief time. This recognition will force us to appreciate our limitations and immerse ourselves in the present without postponing or surfacing. Instead, we will live life to the fullest. It also makes us responsible, without trying to find excuses. Since we are responsible for who we are, how we deal with people and events, our thoughts and feelings, and ultimately how the world is, we must use our words and actions responsibly. Since we are part of this world, our words and actions continuously affect our surroundings, the people we are in touch with, humanity, and our planet. Without this kind of awareness and commitment, we will not be able to ascend the consciousness ladder.

As we have seen, progressing on the path does not entail blocking what we dislike or what bothers us. It will only get repressed, and from our unconscious, it will keep coming back in different disguises. Strategies that we use when faced with external events that annoy us or are unpleasant (e.g. avoiding them and trying to run away from them at all costs) are not effective with internal affairs. Pushing away painful memories or bothersome emotions does not make them go away. It only reinforces them.

If we get attached to our desires and addictions to escape the unpleasantness and difficulties of life, we will end up in trouble. It works when we can see it all without any blinders or filters, and we let it pass as clouds pass through a clear blue sky: no need to resist, no need to grasp. By becoming proficient in doing so, thoughts, emotions, urges and fears lose their grip on us. We become a witness to our own inner and outer reality, and we become our own masters, too.

Detachment gives us freedom. It is an attitude of total involvement and commitment to the path of inner evolution without worrying about the outcome. The ego is haunted by the past through fears, beliefs, regrets, longing, or is preoccupied with the future and what may happen out of its control. The attempt to find security ends in frustration and disappointment because it comes from a place of fear, leading to anxiety and continuous concern—losing the opportunity to go beyond.

The process of disidentifying with the ego does not mean we have to reject it. We are discussing the possibility of achieving greater integration of all aspects of ourselves beyond the previous limitations. So, we can feel our true transpersonal identity instead. The ego is only one part of our larger self, which includes the physical and the material, but also the same universal energy and vital force that composes all consciousness. Without a continuous exercise of mindfulness, we cannot go beyond our reasoning and discursive mind with its inclination to a ceaseless flow of thoughts.

Cultivating mindfulness is what drives us to the present moment. Being aware of what is actually happening without prejudices or personal projections that distort reality and bias our judgment is what can free us from mechanical reactions. This does not mean that wise people do not have impulses. It is just that their actions do not come from automatic negative emotions. Instead, their behavior is always motivated by present awareness, acceptance, kindness, and quiet joy. Awakening changes everything. Causing and avoiding suffering are no longer the primary motivators. They bring serenity and joy.

Mindfulness has to do with the ability to accept, without any judgment, oneself, the current situation, and even how one feels about it. Acceptance of reality does not necessarily mean approving of it. It is simply not being blind to it, not resisting, grasping, or distorting it. The best way to see reality as clearly as possible is to cut through the distortion of our own judgments about it. Acceptance allows us to be like water, flowing down the stream, finding its way through the valleys and mountains alike, going to the clouds when conditions are right, and then coming back to Earth again. It is wiser to be like water, learning to flow with and cooperate with the way things show up rather than resisting reality's actual shape. While keeping our duties, we let go of the self-centeredness, attachment, and obsessions that used to be the core of who we are. Likewise, when we take responsibility for everything that exists inside ourselves, we can handle it without feeling like a victim. It is necessary to enter the silence within and accept things as they are. By accepting that everything completes its cycle and has its own development, including the people closest to us, we are free and set free.

Of course, it takes a long time, perhaps even a lifetime, to eliminate some aspects of ourselves, such as beliefs. The crucial thing is not to be rigidly identified with or attached to them. Provisional opinions are necessary to map the world, but they must always be open to revision. We must keep an open mind and be present, leaving our theories about reality aside. This gives us a direct experience, a mandatory doorway to consciousness.

Therefore, being on the highway toward the highest levels of human development requires a devoted engagement in experiential practices, as all spiritual traditions worldwide have taught. These methods aspire to quieten the mind so that we can perceive directly. They silence the internal dialogue by eliminating false beliefs, dissolving personal importance, and training us to focus on our silent essence that needs no more interpretations about the world. Any form of contemplation and meditation that helps us exercise this is of utmost importance.

Profound books and teachings are great pointers and guides to the right path. Having the advice of others who have already walked the path and kindly stopped to draw a map can significantly assist others that come afterward. I, for one, am incredibly grateful to a few masters who showed me the way. Their journey and the work they generously shared have proven to be fundamental to my own inner voyage. Unfortunately, this is such a rare and arduous path that without the charts those more advanced travelers have drawn, it would be almost impossible to navigate for the rest of us.

However, just reading and theorizing about it will not take us too far. Some glimpses of what it is like to dwell on pure consciousness can be obtained, but do not expect that to lead us to our final destination.

It is not easy to shift our viewpoint to a heightened state of awareness that enables us to see beyond the chatter of the mind and its ideas. It is an enormous challenge to do something we have not done before, and the usual tools we have used to survive and advance in life are useless in this situation. It is challenging to raise our level of consciousness when we do not know what that level is. It takes such a leap in perspective that it may take many years (and even many lives) of inner work to get free of conditioned baggage to cross that threshold.

It usually starts with momentary flashes. They are not permanent, but they allow us to have firsthand experience of what mystics, yogis, and sages have always talked about. They also act as clues about where to evolve our consciousness in the future if we desire. Furthermore, they open our hearts and minds to a new world that words cannot even describe. It is indescribable, beyond words and concepts. As we continue to practice, those moments will appear more often, and for more extended periods until, one day, they become a permanent part of our state of being.

As we discussed in a previous chapter, meditation is an essential entry point because it facilitates dropping out of the continuous inner dialogue and endless interpretation of what happened, what is happening, and what could happen. It allows you to be in touch with a different way of relating to reality, discover some of the various layers that exist, see some of the additional dimensions hidden to the untrained mind, and so on. Perception gets subtler, and one truly understands—through personal experience—that the rational mind is just one tool, but we have many others available.

Yet, meditative states and the increased perception are not relevant in themselves. Meditation is a way to quieten the mind so that we can practice mindfulness all day long, wherever we are and wherever we go. Observe yourself, your thoughts, and your compulsions, and then let them go. To awaken, we need to be anchored in the here and now, releasing identification with the world's changing conditions and with our own history, thoughts, and beliefs. Just resting in that peaceful awareness that encompasses everyone and everything. This would significantly change from the many different temporary states of mind to pure consciousness. As the Advaita Indian master Sri Nisargadatta once explained:

I see, hear and taste as you do, feel hunger and thirst; if lunch is not served on time, even impatience will arise. All this I perceive quite clearly, but somehow I am not in it. There is awareness of it all and a sense of immense distance.

Impatience arises; hunger arises. Even when illness and death of this body arise, they have nothing to do with who I am.

The advancement is not about feeling nothing or becoming frozen; it is about having a shift in identity. And it is impossible to do that without being very mindful and present in the now.

Let's keep in mind that reaching the highest stages of wisdom is not easy. We go against the tide by warning that this requires steady focus, countless renunciations, vast doses of energy and resilience, inner discipline, perseverance, determination, and commitment to work on oneself and plant wholesome seeds wherever we go. The spiritual master Ram Dass described this succinctly: "You may have expected that enlightenment would come instantaneously and permanently. This is unlikely. After the first 'aha' experience, it can be thought of as the thinning of a layer of clouds." Our lower nature and ego compulsions act as a weight that pulls us down and makes it very hard to rise above them. Walking a spiritual path takes considerable effort until it becomes effortless, and we must be aware of it.

Despite all the difficulties and obstacles you will encounter, if you continue on a true spiritual path, you will eventually find a point where you no longer seek but are. Your mind is so full of compassion, contentment, gratitude, spaciousness, presence, and peace that these qualities serve as the transmitters of your soul. The dream of Alchemists through history then takes place in you. You realize that you are everything you ever aspired to be. You are consciousness itself, and everything is part of it too. Everything becomes a vision of constantly changing and evolving perfection that recreates itself through every living creature in this universe and all other universes. Everything appears magical, loving, and whole. You embody grace. And so, the journey continues...

About Mónica Esgueva

Mónica Esgueva is an author, therapist, teacher, and spiritual guide whose work touches people profoundly, inspiring transformations in their day-to-day lives. She has a distinct voice, appealing to people from many backgrounds, showing a path of evolution of consciousness from wherever we are right now.

She is the author of eight self-development books published in Spain and Latin America, including the bestselling *Mindfulness*. She studied with great spiritual masters, such as the Dalai Lama, for ten years in India and Nepal. This has allowed her to combine the best of Eastern and Western thought currents.

She holds a Bachelor's degree in Economics and a Master's degree in Foreign Trade. Afterward, she completed several studies and training in Coaching with NLP (with John Grinder, co-creator of Neuro-Linguistic Programming), in mindfulness at

UCLA, psychology and neurosciences at MIT and King's College London, hypnosis at the NLP Center of New York, and more.

Since 2008, she has worked as a transformational coach and has taught emotional mastery, self-knowledge, and mindfulness to executives in companies such as Accenture, Samsung, and Oracle.

She also teaches workshops, and guides meditation and transcendence retreats. Drawing on her volunteering experience with children with cancer and terminally ill patients, she teaches courses about spiritual preparation for dying. Very committed to guiding others' inner evolution, she works as a past life regression and healing therapist as well.

She was honored as one of the Top 100 Women Leaders in Spain and received one of the Top 10 "Thinkers and Experts Awards" in 2014. Besides her native Spain, she has lived in Paris, London, Tanzania, and Asia. She speaks four languages fluently.

From the author

Thank you for purchasing *The 7 Levels of Wisdom*. I sincerely hope you derived as much from reading this book as I have in creating it. I would be very grateful if you could add a short book review to your favorite online site for feedback. Also, if you would like to book a session with me, find out about forthcoming workshops, read recent blog posts, or sign up for my newsletter, you can do so at monicaesgueva.com. You can also connect with me on Youtube and on Twitter @MonicaEsgueva.

Warmly,
Mónica Esgueva

MANTRA
BOOKS

EASTERN RELIGION & PHILOSOPHY

We publish books on Eastern religions and philosophies. Books
that aim to inform and explore the various traditions that
began in the East and have migrated West.
If you have enjoyed this book, why not tell other readers by
posting a review on your preferred book site.

Recent bestsellers from MANTRA BOOKS are:

The Way Things Are
A Living Approach to Buddhism
Lama Ole Nydahl
An introduction to the teachings of the Buddha, and how to
make use of these teachings in everyday life.
Paperback: 978-1-84694-042-2 ebook: 978-1-78099-845-9

Back to the Truth
5000 Years of Advaita
Dennis Waite
A demystifying guide to Advaita for both those new to, and those
familiar with this ancient, non-dualist philosophy from India.
Paperback: 978-1-90504-761-1 ebook: 978-184694-624-0

Shinto: A celebration of Life
Aidan Rankin
Introducing a gentle but powerful spiritual pathway reconnecting
humanity with Great Nature and affirming all aspects of life.
Paperback: 978-1-84694-438-3 ebook: 978-1-84694-738-4

In the Light of Meditation
Mike George
A comprehensive introduction to the practice of meditation
and the spiritual principles behind it. A 10 lesson meditation
programme with CD and internet support.
Paperback: 978-1-90381-661-5

A Path of Joy
Popping into Freedom
Paramananda Ishaya
A simple and joyful path to spiritual enlightenment.
Paperback: 978-1-78279-323-6 ebook: 978-1-78279-322-9

The Less Dust the More Trust

Participating in The Shamatha Project, Meditation and Science
Adeline van Waning, MD PhD
The inside-story of a woman participating in frontline
meditation research, exploring the interfaces of mind-practice,
science and psychology.
Paperback: 978-1-78099-948-7 ebook: 978-1-78279-657-2

I Know How To Live, I Know How To Die

The Teachings of Dadi Janki: A warm, radical, and life-
affirming view of who we are, where we come from, and what
time is calling us to do
Neville Hodgkinson
Life and death are explored in the context of frontier science
and deep soul awareness.
Paperback: 978-1-78535-013-9 ebook: 978-1-78535-014-6

Living Jainism

An Ethical Science
Aidan Rankin, Kanti V. Mardia
A radical new perspective on science rooted in intuitive
awareness and deductive reasoning.
Paperback: 978-1-78099-912-8 ebook: 978-1-78099-911-1

Ordinary Women, Extraordinary Wisdom

The Feminine Face of Awakening
Rita Marie Robinson
A collection of intimate conversations with female spiritual
teachers who live like ordinary women, but are engaged
with their true natures.
Paperback: 978-1-84694-068-2 ebook: 978-1-78099-908-1

The Way of Nothing
Nothing in the Way
Paramananda Ishaya
A fresh and light-hearted exploration of the amazing reality of
nothingness.
Paperback: 978-1-78279-307-6 ebook: 978-1-78099-840-4

Readers of ebooks can buy or view any of these bestsellers by
clicking on the live link in the title. Most titles are published
in paperback and as an ebook. Paperbacks are available in
traditional bookshops. Both print and ebook formats are
available online.

Find more titles and sign up to our readers' newsletter at
http://www.johnhuntpublishing.com/mind-body-spirit. Follow
us on Facebook at https://www.facebook.com/OBooks and
Twitter at https://twitter.com/obooks.